PARADISE OR HELL?

Mel Ladner

Paradise or Hell?
Copyright © 2022 by Mel Ladner

All rights reserved. No part of this book may be reproduced or transmitted in any form or by any means, electronic or mechanical, including photocopying, recording, or by any information storage and retrieval system without express written permission from the author, except in the case of brief quotations embodied in critical reviews and certain other noncommercial uses permitted by copyright law.

Printed in the United States of America.

Brilliant Books Literary
137 Forest Park Lane Thomasville
North Carolina 27360 USA

Chapter
ONE

Mary and Joseph lived in a rent-controlled railroad apartment in the Coney Island neighborhood of Brooklyn, New York, and were married for six years. They tried to have children without success.

Joseph worked as a New York City bus driver on the cross-town bus on 86th Street in Manhattan from 8:00 AM to 4:30 PM. It was the busiest time of the day, with horrendous traffic and large crowds of pedestrians who liked to cross in the middle of the street or against traffic lights. Only with God's help did Joseph avoid running over jaywalkers or having an accident.

Mary worked as a registered nurse at Mount Sinai Hospital in Manhattan.

They consulted with top doctors for pregnancy tests and to ask what procedures to try for Mary to become pregnant. All the tests indicated they couldn't have children.

At dinner, Mary brought up the subject. "Joseph, we've been trying to have a child for the last six years. I'll be forty this coming December. I might be too old to conceive. Maybe we should adopt."

"You read my mind, Mary. Let's get a lawyer and see if we can adopt a child. Even if we have to take out a loan to pay for it, it would be worth it. We would give any child a loving home and would make very caring parents."

"I love you, Joseph! I have a contact at the hospital who deals with unwanted children who need homes. I'll contact her tomorrow to see what we have to do to start the adoption process. Maybe we won't need a lawyer."

The next day, Mary called Cathy, a friend who was also the director of social workers at the hospital. Cathy's job was to help people cope with everyday problems, including finding families for unwanted children.

"Hello, Cathy. It's Mary."

"It's great to hear from you. How's Joseph doing? What can I do for you?"

"He's well, but we're having trouble conceiving a child. I had a long talk with him, and we've decided to adopt. Can you advise us how to go through that process?"

"I've known you two for a long time. You have a wonderful relationship and would make great parents. Should I come to your floor in the hospital, or do you want to come down here to fill out the forms. There's a long waiting list for adoptions."

"I have a couple questions first."

"Go ahead. I'll try to answer."

"Do we need a lawyer for an adoption? Do we get to choose the child before we adopt? How long does it take to complete an adoption?"

"Most of the time you'll need a lawyer, but since I know you, I can have the hospital attorney do the papers for free. It can take years to complete the adoption process, but I can help with that, too.

"I have a child available who's two-weeks old, a boy with brown eyes and dark complexion who might be from the Middle East. He was abandoned at birth. We call him Saul. He's in the hospital nursery without parents.

"The strange part about him is we don't know where he came from. He was just there in the nursery yesterday. Nobody saw anyone bring him in. It was like he appeared from nowhere. This is pretty embarrassing for the staff, because there are no papers or procedures being followed. You could do all of us a big favor and claim him as yours."

"We're definitely interested. How should we go about this adoption?"

"There's no record of his birth. We checked with all the hospital staff and had our security people investigate any reports for a missing baby.

There weren't any reports anywhere in the country. Where he came from is still a mystery.

"One clue, though, is he has a necklace with a bronze medallion of a <u>fish.</u> On the floor beside the baby was a cloth pouch filled with ancient Roman coins. I spoke to the hospital administrator, and he wants us to give the baby away as soon as possible without the usual paperwork. If you want to adopt him, it'll be a secret between us and the hospital. We'll fill out the forms as if you delivered the baby yourself, and we'll give you a birth certificate, too. That way, he'll be legally yours."

"I don't want him to know he was adopted when he grows up. My nosy neighbors would tell Paul he was adopted, and the last thing we want is to hurt his feelings."

"We named him Saul, but you can change that to Paul if you want. Can you move away from Coney Island and buy a house in a new neighborhood, so nobody would know he was adopted?"

"I like Paul better, so from now on, the baby's name should be Paul. There's no rush to move. Paul won't be able to talk to anyone for a couple years."

"Let's go to the private hospital room where Paul's being kept. I'll introduce you to your new son. Come to my office to meet me."

Mary went to the office and helped Cathy stand up and walk to the elevator.

"Thank you, Mary," Cathy said. "I've been having trouble walking lately, and my eyesight isn't very good. I've been getting severe headaches and have trouble sleeping, but I have no choice but to work to pay my bills."

"I'm sorry to hear you're having such problems," Mary said, concerned. "If there's anything I can do, let me know."

"Thanks for your concern, but there's nothing to be done. I'm in God's hands. Let's go see Paul."

"I can't wait!"

They took the elevator to the private hospital suite on the top floor. As they entered the room, Mary saw the baby and immediately fell in love with him. She felt a burning passion, as if she were in the presence of God. An aura of light surrounding the baby streamed in through a window, reminding her of a painting done by Michelangelo on the Sistine Chapel.

"I want to adopt him," Mary said. "Can I take him home today?"

"Don't you want to call Joseph to see if he approves first?"

"He's working," she said excitedly, "and I can't reach him. I know he'd approve. What do I have to do to take Paul home?"

"Wow, Mary. That's a quick decision. Think it over for a moment. I need to call the hospital director and our attorney. They want to get rid of the baby quickly, so I doubt there's any trouble with the adoption. Stay here. I'll be back as soon as possible with their decision."

Cathy left, and Mary was alone with Paul. Picking him up to hold him for the first time, she felt an immediate attachment. While cuddling him in her arms, she couldn't take her eyes off him, and she felt a bond growing with the child. He had brown hair and eyes, a dark complexion, and seemed to be normal in size and weight.

Paul opened his eyes and seemed as if he attempted to communicate with her. She talked to him and suddenly had a daydream, where a burst of light surrounded her. She saw herself in a white satin robe with a rainbow of light around her head. She stood in a beautiful garden filled with vivid colors in white, blue, red, with a 200-foot waterfall behind her. The sound of the water was peaceful, and she wondered if that was what the Garden of Eden looked like.

A deep male voice spoke to her in Hebrew. She wondered if it was God speaking to her.

Confused, she stiffened and closed her eyes. "Lord, I don't speak Hebrew. I'm a Christian."

The voice immediately changed to English. "I am the Lord thy God. Trust in Me with all your heart and lean not on your own understanding in all your ways. Acknowledge Me, and I shall direct you onto the correct path. Mary, you and baby Jesus, along with Joseph, have been chosen to end the chaos, war, poverty, starvation, sickness, greed, and corruption that permeate the world I created.

"Love the Lord your God with all your heart and with all your soul and with all your strength and with all your mind. Love your neighbor as yourself.

"I will speak to you in dreams to direct you on what you must do to achieve peace and save the world I created. You'll be able to adopt baby Jesus and bring him home today. The Second Coming of Jesus Christ has begun. Baby Jesus is a direct disciple of the Lord, put on earth and into your care to cleanse the world of its demons."

Mary, trying to shake off the daydream, failed. She concentrated on the image and what the Lord said.

"Take baby Jesus to your home. He'll bring together the most-hated men in the world, those who are directed by Satan. He seduced them, filling them with falsehoods and sin. Jesus will drive Satan and his demons out of those men and any of their followers. They will praise the work of Jesus and drop their weapons, seeking peace once they meet baby Jesus. He will save the world. All My children will live in peace for 1,000 years, and there will be a new paradise on earth. The world will be called the New Jerusalem."

"I'm confused over Paul's name, Lord. What do You want me to do?"

"This is the Second Coming of Jesus Christ. Your baby is named Jesus Christ. I direct you and Joseph to give baby Jesus a good home, be good Christians, and to spread My word. Prepare the world for the coming of paradise on earth. Jesus will know when the time is right to meet the most-hated men in the world and rid them of their demons."

Mary, bowing, made the sign of the cross. "Lord, I will obey You."

She awoke from her daydream and found herself with Jesus in her arms. She looked at the child in confusion, trying to make sense of what just happened. She and Joseph had just been given the mission of saving the world.

Cathy walked into the room with a handful of papers. "Sorry it took so long. I've been speaking with the hospital director and our top lawyer. They agree you can adopt the baby today. Just sign these adoption papers, and you can take Paul home.

"All of them told me they had a dream last night when the Lord spoke to them, directing them to allow baby Jesus to be adopted by you and Joseph. I don't know what to make of that, but they said the baby's real name is Jesus, not Paul."

Her voice became urgent and frightened. "Please sign all these forms. I'll notarize them to make them legal. The name on the forms is Jesus Christ, not Paul. I don't know how that was done, but I can't change it back."

"I had a dream, too," Mary said. "I met our Lord and called the baby Paul, but He said the name should be Jesus Christ. I love that name. Could it be that this baby is the Second Coming of our Lord to save the world? I believe it is."

With shaking hands, Cathy held out the forms and a gold pen. Mary held Jesus in her left arm and didn't bother reading the papers. She just signed them and handed them back, so Cathy could notarize them.

Mary looked at Jesus, who had a beautiful smile. His expression showed that he understood what Mary was doing.

After Cathy notarized the forms, she turned to Mary and the baby. "Congratulations. Baby Jesus is legally your son. You can take him home today."

Mary held the child tightly. "Thank You, Lord, for this gift."

"I'll be right back. I must make copies of these papers to be filed in our office. I'll give you the originals for safekeeping. Thank you for adopting this baby. You did us all a big favor. The hospital would be in trouble if news of this leaked, and we couldn't explain where the baby came from. We might even lose our license."

Cathy left to make copies, and suddenly, the door opened to reveal a tall, blind Muslim in a white robe. He held a copy of the Quran in his left hand.

"Am I in the right room?" he asked.

"Which room do you want?" Mary asked.

"Is this room 1825?"

"No. this is 1801. We can take you to 1825 if you wish."

"Is that a baby I hear? He has a very nice voice. I'll bet he's beautiful. Can I sit down? I had a dream where I stood in a beautiful garden with a clear water fall at least 200-feet tall falling into a peaceful river. In the background was a magnificent mosque."

She saw the man sweating profusely, but his expression was peaceful. "Please, sit down."

He touched a chair beside the hospital bed and sat silently. Different expressions moved across his face, as if he were talking to someone in his mind. He kept nodding as if agreeing.

"I believe I just spoke to the Lord," he said. "He called me my full name in a deep, beautiful voice, and he used quotes from the Quran. He has directed me to spread the word and to follow my God to achieve peace, tolerance, and prosperity in this world. He directed me to attend mosque service regularly and tell ten people at the mosque, who will each tell ten more, and so on. All will be told to follow their God and attend mosque services, helping to spread the word of God for total peace, tolerance, and prosperity in our world.

"The Lord told me to prepare for the coming of the new world, which will be called the New Jerusalem, a paradise on earth."

As he sat in the chair, he suddenly blinked his eyes and shouted, "I can see! I can see!"

Staff members rushed into the room at the sound of his voice. The resident doctor who'd been treating the man examined him, while others watched in amazement.

The doctor took out a magnifying glass and checked the man's eyes, then he held a coin in his right hand. "Look at this coin."

The blind man looked at it and smiled. "It's a quarter."

The nine people in the room gasped, then all fell silent. A moment later, they took out their cell phones and started live streaming news of the miracle.

The blind man took the quarter in his hand and studied it. "This was printed in 1982, and the words on the back are 'In God we trust.'"

The doctor shook his head. "I can't explain this. There's no medical explanation for how he regained his eyesight."

Mary held Jesus in her arms and said, "We've been chosen to save the souls of all the believers who attend their houses of worship, believe in God, and follow Him. We will achieve peace on earth. This means the end of chaos, war, poverty, starvation, sickness, greed, and corruption. The Lord has directed us to believe in Him. There's only one God in all the universe. All religions interpret that God in different spiritual, behavioral, and practical ways. That's the foundation for the different religions.

"The Second Coming of Jesus will show all believers there is only one God, and it will reunite all religions into one to work for peace, tolerance, equal rights, and paradise on earth. God asks that all demons and good people in the world must become believers in the almighty God. They must attend their places of worship regularly and follow His word.

"The Lord told me to pass this message on to the world, 'Love the Lord your God with all your heart, and with all your soul, and with all your strength, and with all your mind. Love your neighbor as yourself.'

"In the Lord's name, I direct each of you to tell ten people, who will each tell ten more, and so on, about the miracle you have seen. Attend your churches, mosques, and temples regularly to spread the Lord's word of peace."

She saw a Jewish Rabbi in a wheelchair. Mary motioned him to come to the front of the room. He did, assisted by a nurse.

Mary approached the man with baby Jesus in her arms. "Rabbi, can you walk?"

"No. I'm paralyzed from the waist down. I haven't walked since an auto accident ten years ago. There's no hope I'll ever walk again."

"We're directed by our Lord that if you promise to follow your God and spread His word to achieve peace, tolerance, and prosperity to the people of your faith and to other religions, baby Jesus will cure you. You will walk again."

"I promise you and the Lord I will speak at my synagogue and tell ten people, who will each tell ten more, to spread the word of our Lord for peace on earth."

"Hold baby Jesus in your arms and relax in your wheelchair. Close your eyes and listen to what the Lord tells you."

Mary placed the baby in the rabbi's arms. He studied the baby and saw its expression become peaceful. After a moment, he returned the baby to Mary and then seemed to fall asleep. His lips moved, but no one heard him speak. He nodded as if agreeing to something.

Twenty minutes later, he woke with a smile that showed clearly through his long, gray beard. Grasping the arms of the wheelchair, he stood and shouted in Hebrew, "Thank You, Lord!"

He turned to Mary and recounted a similar vision to the one she and the blind man had, of a garden of paradise, where the rabbi wore a white satin robe.

"The Lord spoke to me, calling me by my full name in Hebrew. He quoted the Old Testament. He said there is only one God, and that all religions follow Him. God has directed me to spread His word to my congregation and the world."

He walked to the blind Muslim man, who stared out the window at beautiful Central Park. The blind man turned at his approach, opened his arms, and hugged him.

"Peace, tolerance, and prosperity on earth!" they said in unison.

Mary turned to the others in the room. "We've been directed by the Lord to have you swear to Him that you'll follow His wishes to help create peace, tolerance, and prosperity in the world. You must follow your own religions and attend worship services regularly. You will help spread the Lord's word in your churches, temples, and mosques."

Cathy tried to force her way through the crowd with the adoption forms for Mary, but she couldn't get through the number of people in the hall. Doctors and patients wanted to see Mary and ask for help curing various ailments.

"What's going on here?" Cathy asked. "Is everyone OK?"

The chief ophthalmologist said, "We just witnessed two miracles. Mary and baby Jesus cured a blind man and a paraplegic. I'm not a religious person, but I'll be in church every Sunday from now on. I'm a believer now. I promise to spread the Lord's word for peace, tolerance, and prosperity."

He shoved his way through the crowd, checking his pockets for money. He took out all his cash, $666.00, and found a young pregnant woman who recently came to the hospital, although she was too poor to afford treatment, and gave her the money.

The people in the room cheered and applauded.

"Peace and tolerance on earth!" they shouted.

"God bless you," the pregnant woman said. "You can count on me and my baby to do whatever we can to create paradise on earth."

Cathy was dumbfounded. The meanest, most-hated doctor in the hospital, who never showed any concern for others, just exhibited an act of love, tolerance, and kindness to a stranger.

Cathy finally made it through the crowd and met the ophthalmologist. "What's happening in here?"

"We witnessed two miracles," he said. "The man standing behind you was in a wheelchair with no hope of walking, but after baby Jesus and Mary told him to speak to the Lord, he went into a dream. When he awoke, he could stand and walk!

"Before we got here, the man who's staring out the window right now was blind. He was cured, too, after he spoke to the Lord.

"I've been practicing medicine for a very long time, and I never saw anything like this. These are miracles. That's all they can be!"

"I don't believe in miracles," Cathy said. "It must be a trick."

Mary waved her hand to bring Cathy closer, then she pushed her way through the room to reach Cathy. "Do you have the original forms?"

Cathy handed them to her.

Mary studied them and nodded. "Thank you, Cathy, for everything. I see you doubt the miracles the Lord has performed through baby Jesus. Let me introduce you to your Lord. Have a seat on the edge of the bed."

Cathy gingerly sat on the bed. "Is this some kind of joke? Talking to the Lord? I haven't practiced my Catholic faith in years."

"Give yourself to the Lord, and you shall be rewarded. Sit down and close your eyes."

Cathy did and immediately fell asleep. Her expression changed from a frown to a smile. She nodded slowly once or twice.

The crowd grew larger, as more and more people heard the news. Some took pictures and texted about Cathy in her dream state.

A hush fell. Cathy woke in twenty-five minutes, opened her eyes, and looked around the room. Her account of the dream was the same as the others.

"I can't believe He called me by full name!" she said. "I felt like He knew me! He spoke in Latin and English, quoting the New Testament. I saw a beautiful waterfall and a gorgeous park with the prettiest flowers I ever saw. A tall church stood in the background with a steeple that reached all the way to the sky."

She stood and held her head in her hands. "I have no headache! My vision is clear! I feel fine. I didn't want the administration to know I was diagnosed with brain cancer. I've been dealing with it for nine months. Can it be my cancer has been cured? Thank You, Lord!"

One of the doctors who'd been treating her took her hand. "Let's run some tests and see if you're cancer free."

Cathy turned to Mary and the baby. "Thank You. I fell in love with my Lord and will attend church every Sunday and practice my Catholic faith. I promise to work for peace, tolerance, and prosperity."

She walked out with the doctor.

The miracles immediately went viral on Twitter and the Internet. Soon, over six billion hits were recorded, as people watched the miracles being performed.

Mary, holding baby Jesus in her arms, turned toward a man, whose laptop was feeding a video of events in the room to the Internet. "We are directed by our Lord to tell you to follow your God. Love your neighbor as thyself. Make the world peaceful and show tolerance. God bless you."

After that feed went out to the Internet, Mary heard a crowd roaring outside the hospital. Within minutes, TV news trucks and newspaper reporters arrived. The New York City Police Department was dispatched to control the crowd, as people came in alone or with family members to seek cures for their illnesses.

Within an hour, over 100,000 people were gathered outside. The crowd quickly got out of hand, and a riot ensued. The police called for assistance, and more officers came in to quell the riot.

The phone in the hospital room rang. A doctor answered and heard the voice of the President.

"May I talk to Mary?" he asked.

"Yes, Mr. President." He gave the receiver to Mary, who still held Jesus in her arms. "It's the President of the United States!" he whispered.

The room fell silent.

"Yes, Mr. President?" Mary asked.

"I've been watching you and baby Jesus live on the Internet. If what I saw is true, you have the power from the Lord to make our world a paradise. You can count on the United States and all our allies to help you achieve your goal. I have sent members of the Secret Service to guard you and the baby. They'll arrive shortly."

"I don't think we need protection. We're in the Lord's hands, doing His work."

Joseph finally waded through the crowd to reach the room where Mary was. He came in while she spoke to the President and went to greet his new son. Joseph, holding the baby in his arms, fell in love instantly.

"Mary, there are evil people out there who want to do Satan's work. They're the opponents of all mankind, terrorizing our world. They'll stop at nothing to prevent us from having paradise."

"Mr. President, the Lord has told us how to achieve our goal of paradise on earth and to rid ourselves of the demons who inhabit our world. We must refuse the protection of the Secret Service. Thank you for your concern over our safety, but we must put our trust in the Lord."

"All right. I'll respect your decision. I promise all nations in the free world will use our power to fulfill the Lord's will. I'd love to have you and your family here at the White House to meet with me and other world leaders to plan how to achieve this goal. Once we agree on a location for the meeting, I'll be in touch.

"I believe Satan will try to stop us with every weapon in his arsenal. He'll use his servants who occupy important positions on earth to attack us. With the help of the Lord and all people of good faith, we'll win and have paradise."

"I agree with you, Mr. President. With all people of good faith working together, we can defeat Satan and his followers. You set the date for the peace meeting, and we'll be there. God bless you."

"I'll be in touch in a few days."

Mary hung up.

"What did he say?" someone shouted.

"Thank God the President is a man who has faith in the Lord. He's on our side to create heaven on earth and defeat all evil people."

There was a commotion at the back of the crowd. A heavily muscled man who looked like a linebacker for a football team, came in wearing a black Sikh turban. His black leather jacket had slogans against Christians, Muslims, and Jews, as well as the words, *Satan Is Great!*

Pulling out a large knife, he tried to slash people in the crowd. Joseph and others subdued him and held him down before he hurt anyone.

"My name is Cain," he growled. "I've been instructed via the Internet to kill all those who don't follow Satan. We'll use suicide bombers, mass shootings, beheadings, or anything else we can to prevent people from living in harmony! That is Satan's will!"

Mary watched Cain hold the man in a headlock. Someone else took the knife from the man's hand.

"Why do you hate us so?" Mary demanded. "Why would you want to stop a movement for peace, tolerance, and prosperity? Who instructed you on the Internet to kill us?"

"It came over the live-recorded stream. Satan declared war on all you believers. I was sent here by Satan to stop the second coming of Jesus Christ and to tell the world that there's a war against peace, tolerance, and prosperity in the world. All believers will be destroyed.

"You'll witness mass killing of innocent victims from suicide bombings of schools, airports, train stations, movie theaters, and other places. You can't imagine the pain and suffering the good people in the world will endure. We'll even use nuclear weapons against the believers in this world. You and your Lord can't stop Satan and his followers from killing all believers!"

"Yes, we can. The Lord of all sent baby Jesus here to stop the madness of killing good people who don't agree with Satan and his demon followers.

Mary motioned to Joseph to bring baby Jesus to the man being held on the floor. Cain fought hard, possessed by the demons he carried.

Mary held Jesus over Cain's face, while all the iPhones and cameras in the room transmitted the event. Mary turned toward those recording the moment and said, "I'll show you and the world the power of our Lord."

Cain refused to look at Mary and Jesus. He turned his head away, jerking it from side-to-side to avoid Jesus' gaze. Finally, Cain closed his eyes to avoid looking, but he fell into a deep sleep. His body went limp, and his angry expression became blissful. His head slowly moved from side-to-side.

He seemed to be holding two different conversations. His lips moved, but no one heard any words.

After fifty-five minutes, Cain woke up and turned to Mary, who still held baby Jesus. "My name has changed. From now on, call me Abel. Please bring baby Jesus to me. I have a message from our Lord to all the good people in the world."

The people in the room stared in shock. Mary approached Abel while carrying the baby. Four security guards still held Abel down, with his hands handcuffed behind his back.

He looked up at Mary and Jesus. "I just spoke to our Lord and Satan. They were in a large courtroom with a jury of holy men, leaders of all religions of the world.

"Our Lord sat on a high, long, wooden bench. The room held two wooden tables facing each other on opposite sides of the room. On the right was a beautiful female archangel named Julia in a white satin robe who represented our Lord. At the table on the left sat Lucifer to represent Satan. He was five-feet-two-inches tall and wore a black military uniform with two rows of demon medals on the left.

"I was in the witness stand, with our Lord as the judge. When I looked at Him, he wore my image. When I looked at Lucifer, he resembled Adolf Hitler. Archangel Julia and all the men and women in the jury looked like everyday people.

"After hearing the arguments from Archangel Julia and Lucifer, I was cross-examined by the beautiful archangel. Lucifer was sweating and looked old and disheveled in his uniform. After all the witnesses were heard, the evidence presented, and the closing arguments given, I had to decide who was right and wrong.

"I reached my verdict and said our Lord was right. He ruled I made the correct decision. We deserved to live in peace, tolerance, and prosperity in the world. Then our Lord spoke to me.

"'Cain, you are now a messenger of the Lord. Your name will be changed to Abel to show the people of the world they should attend their houses of worship and follow their God to achieve peace on earth and to reject Satan. Protect and defend baby Jesus, Mary, and Joseph from any harm foreign or domestic.'

"He wants me to tell the world that the Earth is the stage, and the universe is the theater. The universe is watching to see what happens to achieve peace on Earth. If we fail, the universe will be destroyed.

"I swore allegiance to our Lord and will do everything in my power to achieve peace, tolerance, and prosperity in our world and protect baby Jesus from harm, so help me God."

Mary, looking at the others in the room, faced those who held up their phones to live stream the event. "Our Lord has spoken through Satan's representative that all humans in the world have a choice to follow our Lord or Satan. All of us have good angels and bad demons in our souls. Everyone must decide who to follow. That choice is yours—good or evil. I beg you to follow our Lord or see our world destroyed.

"There's only one Lord in the world. Humans have given Him different names, but you can see that there's only one Lord we follow. We use different names and follow different cultural behaviors and practices.

We read different holy books, but these bring only one conclusion—there is only one God we all follow.

"Some of our religions have incorrectly interpreted God's word. For instance, the Catholic Church believes nuns and priests can't marry, but we created that law. God never gave such an order to forbid their marriage.

"Muslims have been misled to believe they must kill infidels. That is totally false. God has ordered all believers in Him to live in harmony and peace.

"Followers of Judaism have been misled by the idea that men and women must be segregated in the synagogues during services. God has told us that all are equal in His eyes. We are equal regardless of sex, color, wealth, or sexual orientation. He has given us free reign to do what we wish in the world He created. We have failed, as anyone can see by the wars, murders, and prejudices people have experienced.

"Our Lord has given Satan and those who are possessed by demons to rid themselves of those demons. If they don't, they will end their existence. Religious good people will win and will expel the demons from the bad people in the world. The second coming of baby Jesus will end Satan's rule of Earth. The planet will be cleansed of demons and will be called New Jerusalem. We will live in paradise on Earth. Our Lord has promised this.

"Imagine what believers can achieve if everyone in the world prayed simultaneously for peace and harmony. God's plan is to have the New Jerusalem and the entire universe follow the same time, which will be Greenwich mean time. For example, 9:00 AM in New York City will be 2:00 PM. That's when the workday will begin, and it will end at 10:00 PM GMT. We will no longer follow different clocks. GMT will be used throughout the universe.

"That will make it easy for God to communicate with all good believers in the universe and tell them when to meet at their houses of worship. This permanent time change will begin in seven days.

"God will have all believers go to sleep at their usual times. He will order them to follow His commands while they dream and go to their houses of worship immediately after they hear three loud trumpets sound in their dreams.

"If the believers follow God's order and attend their houses of worship, it will mean the end of Satan's rule. God has promised us paradise on Earth in the New Jerusalem."

The hospital was jammed with people. The crowd outside swelled to over a million, all trying to gain entrance and meet baby Jesus and Mary. Heads of state tried to call Mary and Joseph to receive instructions from the Lord.

"Release Abel from his handcuffs," Mary told the guards.

They did, and he slowly got up to sit in a chair in the corner. "Satan is wrong," he declared. "I believe in my heart we should have peace, tolerance, and prosperity in our world. I ask you and God for your forgiveness. I promise God I will be your protector for life if you let me."

"Abel, you have made us proud by seeing the light," Mary said. "This should be an example to the world that we as individuals have the choice to follow Satan or our Lord to work toward peace, tolerance, and prosperity. We will create thousands of years of peace on Earth. We as a family accept you as our protector."

She walked over to Abel, still holding Jesus in her arms, and hugged him while kissing his cheek. The room erupted in cheers. Those outside began cheering so loud, it felt like the sound a huge crowd makes in a football stadium.

"We want peace!" the crowd chanted. "New Jerusalem!"

On the TV in the room, they saw the replay of what happened in the room a few minutes earlier being aired to the entire world. More and more people flooded the streets, forming a sea of humanity willing to follow their Lord to achieve peace on Earth.

Chapter
TWO

Satan

Satan and a group of his followers that formed the demonic congress that ruled the world, watched the TV broadcast in shock. Satan had once been called Lucifer, but he became a fallen archangel who changed his name in his attempt to replace God and rule the world. He was limited by being able to be in only one place at a time, and he couldn't transport instantly from one place to another. He also still had access to the Lord.

Satan looked old and decrepit, with a ruddy complexion of fair skin, a dark-black goatee, and a black mustache. He sweated during the broadcast. When he spoke, he always shouted, and he often muttered to himself in words that made little sense. He was filled with restless energy that made him pace a lot. Being in his presence made people fear for their lives.

He was covered from head to toe in a dirty, gray, torn robe and old Roman sandals. His face was difficult to focus on, and two large bumps on his forehead resembled horns. A long lion's tail protruded from under his robe.

His facial features were ugly, with a saddle, flat-bridged nose and only two malformed teeth in his mouth, jutting down from his upper jaw on either side like elephant tusks. His foul odor permeated the room. Looking at him and inhaling that smell often made people sick.

His congress hall was in an underground cavern over 200 feet below the surface. The entrance came out in a large farm on Devil's Mountain that was impossible to scale. Bizarre weather brought constant lightning and tornados to the mountain, and no roads led to the top. Only demons visited the farm.

The demons had a special entrance to the demon cave, which took three days to reach. Demons making the journey took a bus that dropped them off at a submarine on a lake, then they went into an underground tunnel guarded by demon soldiers who had orders to shoot anyone who wasn't a demon.

At least eight times a year, Satan had training drills at the tunnel entrance. He liked to surprise the soldiers with people who were sentenced to execution, ordering them to be released so he could watch the soldiers kill them. Any demon who failed to attack would be executed by Satan in front of the congress.

In the early 1700s, a few hunters who reached the top of Devil's Mountain were butchered. Searchers later found only their heads. The bones had all the flesh stripped from them. It was such a gruesome scene, people began to whisper that the devil lived on that mountain, and no one was willing to climb it ever again. Anyone who tried to climb it died horribly.

Detectives who were sent up the mountain to investigate the murders were killed by lightning and tornados. Their bodies were never recovered. The legend that the devil lived up there grew over the years.

One man fell from the mountaintop and lived long enough to tell people that he saw Satan just before he was struck by lightning. He described Satan as disheveled and dirty, wearing torn black rags for clothing. He didn't see Satan's face, but he described two small horns on his forehead and a lion's tail. Satan's stench was perceptible from 100 meters.

Residents in the area accepted the fact that no one could climb Devil's Mountain. The government posted signs that read, *Danger. Enter Devil's Mountain at Your Own Risk!*

Over generations, people accepted the legend that the mountain was off limits to everyone.

To enter the demon's congress hall, the demon Senators had to enter the large farmhouse and descend steps that led 200 feet down. The temperature dropped until the rail and the stairs were damp with moisture. Puddles of water were everywhere.

As they went deeper into the cavern, they found the ceiling and floors covered with stalactites and stalagmites. Water dripping constantly covered the cavern floor.

The demon congressmen wore raincoats, as they sat at their desks. They had towels available to wipe water off their heads and faces.

The cavern was carved into a large, windowless hall with a black granite podium facing the leaders. Eight desks were spaced around the hall with TVs and computers on them, from which the demons watched the events in the hospital room with Mary and baby Jesus. The demons represented the seven continents of Asia, Africa, North America, South America, Antarctica, Europe, Australia, and the South Pole.

The large congressional hall had a round black marble floor that was wet and slippery. The décor was similar to the Roman senate of Constantinople. Hanging on the walls of the Senate were thousands of portraits in waterproof frames of the worst people in world history. Behind Satan's podium was a portrait of Adolf Hitler and Jeffery Dahmer in two large, golden, waterproof picture frames.

Each member of the congress could vote on how to achieve chaos, poverty, unrest, and misery in the world. Satan, who always had the final vote, could veto anything the demon congress passed. Each Senator had a congressional staff of over 1,000 demons. Demons were recruited to work for the Senators based on the evil deeds they performed in the world. There were so many candidates to choose from, there was a ten-year waiting list.

While waiting for Satan to call the congress to order, the Senators ate a gourmet lunch called *humanda* at their desks. It consisted of the remains of demons who failed in the missions assigned by Satan. Their bodies were carved up with a bone saw, and the remains were fed through a meat grinder prepared by the most-famous chefs in the world, accompanied by exotic ingredients and fancy side dishes and the most-expensive wines. The demon congress gave the meal a five-star rating, calling it "the best chicken dinner you ever had."

After the demons finished toasting each other and eating their lunch, Satan called them to order to show them what happened to Cain, who'd been sent to kill Mary and Joseph but failed.

"We've been waiting for the day to come when Jesus Christ returns as the savior for the believers," Satan said. "We have prepared, and now the day has arrived. If we lose, we face total defeat and will see peace on Earth for thousands of years.

"We'll have a tough time keeping the demons of the world in line. We must find a plan to stop the peace movement, or we'll be doomed to live our lives in peace and harmony."

The Senators gasped, then they shouted, "Kill the believers!"

"Take your seats." Satan rapped the gavel. "The senate will come to order."

Silence fell. He looked at the senate floor and then at the Senator from Africa, Idi Amin, who waved his hand, asking to be recognized to speak. He was born in 1925 in Kobosko, Uganda, and became President of Uganda only to show himself as a brutal dictator who killed millions while he was in power. His lavish lifestyle contributed to the bankruptcy and collapse of his country's economy.

Satan nodded, and Senator Idi Amin stood to speak.

"Satan, members of the Senate, and staff," he began. "The people of peace have declared war against us. I move that we vote on a declaration of war to defend our way of life. <u>The people of peace want to treat us like women are equals to man.</u> That means we will lose our power to control women and treat them like the dogs they are. We must use any means at our disposal to defeat the forces of good and tolerance, or our reign of power will end.

"I've been in contact with our generals for several years, and we already had plans to fight a war against the good people of the world. We will start a guerilla war using human bombs, computer cyber-attacks, propaganda, spreading false news, and rigging elections to place our representatives in office. We will consider any terrorist tactics that this Senate approves.

"We'll put fear of Satan into those believers! We'll blow up their houses of worship and kill as many of the good people as we can. We can storm their public events with suicide demons and kill the attendees. This will bring the good people of the world to their knees and force them to follow us.

"We can use any ideas the Senators come up with to kill as many good people as possible to win the war and install Satan as our god and ruler of the world!

"I move we vote on an act of war." He sat down.

The other Senators stood and cheered except for Senator from South America, Augusto Pinochet, a former President of Chile who murdered over 80,000 people, tortured 30,000 more, and left a legacy of 3,095 people who disappeared and were never found.

Senator Augusto Pinochet raised his hand to speak.

"Senator Pinochet from South America," Satan said, "you're recognized to speak. You have three minutes."

"I've been watching the power of the Lord," Senator Pinochet began, "and I don't believe we can win. I object to the plan to rig the elections run by the good people. Have you read the nonfiction book by Mel Ladner entitled *Human Error?* It spells out the fact that most of their elections are already rigged. We don't have to do a damn thing to rig those. They're doing it for us.

"Perhaps we should try to negotiate a peace treaty with the Lord. I would like to see if we can have peace, tolerance, and prosperity in the world."

Satan stood and screamed, then he shouted, "Seize Pinochet and bring him to me!"

Demon guards grabbed Senator Pinochet and threw him to the floor, punching and kicking him, as they handcuffed him and dragged his bleeding, semiconscious form to the base of Satan's podium.

"Have him kneel before me," Satan commanded.

The guards forced him to a kneeling position.

Satan faced the Senate. "Let this be a lesson to all demon followers. If you don't abide by my rule never to negotiate with believers, you face certain, horrible death!" He glared at the Senator. "I have found you guilty of aiding and abetting the believers. That is punishable by death."

Satan turned to an aide. "Bring the fire cage to the Senate room!"

The guards at the back of the hall ran off and returned a few minutes later wheeling in a large, metal cage, parking it before Satan's podium. At one hundred feet by fifty, it was big enough to hold dozens of people. At the bottom of the cage, a fire pit held five redwood trees long as the cage. They were sufficient to keep the fire going for a long time. One guard carried a ten-gallon can full of gasoline and a burning torch.

"Place the Senator into the cage," Satan ordered. "Uncuff him and lock him in."

The guards obeyed, locking the door after tossing the freed Senator inside.

"Spare my life!" he cried. "I've been a good demon all my life. I caused misery and pain to the good people of Chile! Please, Satan, spare me!" Crying, he stared up at the ceiling.

To the amazement and horror of those watching, Senator Pinochet began praying to the Lord.

Satan glared at the others in the room. "You, Traitor Pinochet, have the gall to follow the Lord! Let this be a lesson to all my followers. We're at war with the believers of the world. I demand your total support to defeat the good people of the world. If I don't have it, this fate will be yours. Light the fire!"

Pinochet, falling to his knees, stared up at Satan. "You might kill me, but you'll never win against our Lord and his followers. Yes, I've had a change of heart. I'm a follower of the Lord. We'll defeat you and your demons!"

A guard opened the can of gas and dumped it on the large trees under the cage. Another guard held the torch over his head and looked up at Satan.

"Kill the believer! Kill the believer!" the Senators chanted.

Satan looked at the Senators and nodded to the guard. The fire ignited quickly. Senator Pinochet ran around the cage, trying to avoid the flames.

"Stop the fire!" he begged.

Senators flinched away from the intense heat and smell of burning flesh, as the fire grew. In less than a minute, Pinochet's clothes were on fire, and his screams intensified. He ran back and forth across the cage, trying to climb out but failing. Finally, he fell to the bottom of the cage and went to his knees, then he fell over, as the cage was engulfed in flames. Within eight minutes of the fire being lit, he was dead.

Applause and cheers erupted in the room. Satan let them cheer for over five minutes, then he rapped his gavel to restore order. He let the cage remain in place, as Pinochet's body burned.

"I have decided to order all the demonic people in the world to prepare for a guerilla war against the good people," Satan said. "We begin from week from Sunday. We will use terrorism and international violence to strike fear into the hearts of our enemies and to achieve our aim of true evil in the world. This is a war for our survival. If we are defeated, the world will become a paradise, with peace on Earth. We must win!"

They applauded and cheered again, showing their approval. When the votes were counted, it was unanimous to declare war against the good people of the world.

"Ask Senator Bernie Madoff, our banker, to address the Senate regarding how to finance this war," Satan said.

Bernie Madoff was convicted of the largest financial fraud in U.S. history. He contributed to his son, Mark's, suicide. When Mark learned that his father ran a Ponzi scheme that bankrupted and defrauded thousands of investors of their life savings, he couldn't face life anymore.

Bernie Madoff stood to face the Senate. "May it please the Senate. I have issued the quarterly financial station. The Senators will have the report on their desks. You may read along with me, as I explain parts of it.

"Please turn to page seven. Satan made a profit of $212 billion for the quarter. Let me break down the highlights.

"At the bottom of the page you can see we made a $76-billion-dollar profit from drug dealing. There was an increase of 500% in the large cities of the U.S. and the world, but it was especially strong in New York City, Detroit, and the middle-class suburbs throughout the country. That surprised me. Another surprise was that the state of Maine had an increase of 1,000% in drug profits for the quarter.

"Once we hook the middle-class children on drugs, we have clients until the day they die. It's a win-win situation for Satan and all the demons of the world.

"We also made a nice profit on prescription drugs and medical insurance, especially the $5,000 deductible believers must pay. Most of the demons of the world don't pay for medical insurance but receive it free from the government.

"I want to thank Demon James. Please stand and be acknowledged for your outstanding suggestion for making all the good people of the world suffer and bring misery to their families for having terminal illnesses. They pay extraordinarily high prices for their prescription drugs to stay alive. All the pharmaceutical companies know they can't afford the drugs. The beauty of the plan is that they must choose whether to pay for their life-saving drugs or for food and rent for their families. Most of the good believers choose the latter. The bad news is that most of them suffer and die from their illnesses."

Satan laughed at that.

Demon James stood to a cheering Senate. Demon Bernie Madoff signaled his guards to bring Demon James to the stage. When he stood beside Demon Madoff to face the Senate, James said, "Thank you, Satan, for recognizing my great ideas to stick it to all the good believers who are terminally ill. My idea created misery for millions of good people and their families. We placed demons in key leading positions in all the major pharmaceutical companies in the world.

"Through this plan, we bankrupted over 27% of the world population and caused countless suicides. Unaffordable medicine is the gift that keeps on giving. The profit Satan made on this plan is in the tens of billions of dollars each quarter.

"We must also acknowledge and applaud all the governments that passed the laws to keep medicine unaffordable for terminally ill patients. Without help from our demon politicians, we could never have caused so much misery to the believers."

The Senators stood and gave him a five-minute ovation.

Satan stood, too. "Demon James, approach the table and kneel before me."

Demon James did.

"I, Satan, hereby promote you to the rank of full Colonel in the demon army." Satan pinned a shied on the demon's garment.

He turned to the congress. "We reward demons who do evil work in promoting our evil cause. We torture and kill all demons who make mistakes or don't please me. You have no choice but to follow me."

Demon James left the podium, while Demon Madoff resumed his report.

"The biggest increase in profits for us was in taxes, tolls, fines for intoxicated driving, and tickets for traffic offenses. Our demon politicians keep increasing taxes and tolls. We showed a 10,000% increase in profits this quarter from that segment alone.

"I told Satan an interesting story about a believer who never did anything wrong in his entire life. The only flaw he had was not attending church and worshipping God. If true believers attend their places of worship, work for peace, and obey their God, their souls are saved. It's almost impossible for Satan to ruin them.

"In my story, Lou Cobb received awards for being the best teacher in a very large inner-city school system. He always volunteered to help the sick and disadvantaged. He had a loving family. We investigated him for years, and he never made a mistake. Finally, though, we had an opportunity to ruin his life and that of his family.

"He went to a teacher's retirement party and drank four rumrunners. Feeling he was too drunk to drive, he slept in the back seat hoping he would wake up and feel OK to drive again.

"The police officers in a car patrolling the neighborhood were called by a demon who complained about a drunk driver in the back seat of his car. We gave them the license plate number and location where the car was parked.

"The police pulled up behind the parked car and walked up to it, seeing someone sleeping in the back seat. They woke him up and asked, 'Do you have the car keys?'

"The man replied, 'Yes, but I didn't drive the car. I slept in the back seat and hoped I would be sober when I woke up.'

"'We got a complaint about this car. Under state law, if you're in possession of your car keys and are in the car, even if the engine is turned off, you can be charged with drunk driving.' They arrested the man."

Loud cheers came from his audience. Even Satan was engrossed in the tale.

"The believer was arrested and taken to jail. He had to pay an attorney over $15,000 in legal fees but still lost his license. He had to attend classes to regain his license, which cost him another $1,000. He also lost his job as a schoolteacher.

"Now for the best part of the story. He became bankrupt, and he and his family were homeless. In New York state, we've had our demon politicians pass a three-strike law that if someone was convicted three times for drunk driving, he would have his license revoked in all fifty states. It is a retroactive law, just to make sure the believers' lives will be ruined forever."

The demon congress stood and cheered.

"We have over ten million believers who don't attend churches or houses of worship, but they still stand out for the good work they do for their fellow men. Demon investigators have them under surveillance, so when the right opportunity comes to ruin one of their lives, a demon can act. Sometimes, we lie to the press to set up believers or plant evidence for a crime. We make false accusations against believers, and the justice system has a 96% conviction rate. Once we get a believer into the justice system, he is usually convicted of a major crime, then we can ruin his life and those of his family members. After their lives are ruined, they come around and learn evil ways in prison until they start following Satan. It's a policy that has worked well for us since Adam and Eve."

Satan laughed and applauded, as Bernie Madoff finished the story. The Senate stood to give Satan a standing ovation to show their approval.

"Our best achievements for profit and power is the female sex slave business," Bernie continued. "We record the audio and video of those sex-slave encounters with clients. The number of married politicians and famous people who were filmed paying to do sex acts is astonishing.

"The best part is, we make a nice profit by blackmailing them to the point they become demons. We have them in our pockets, and they take orders directly from Satan. It's a win-win situation that we love.

"Now for our expenses. We took a hit this quarter on all the kickback we had to give to our demon corrupt politicians. Then there's payout money to rig most of the world's elections. The politicians we have in office will pay us dividends with the taxes, laws, and regulations they will pass that benefit Satan, taking money from hard-working believers and making their lives miserable. Once a law is passed, it's almost impossible to get rid of it. That's another win-win for Satan.

"We have more than enough money to finance the war on the believers. With our experience and evil talent, the war will be over in weeks."

Bernie handed the microphone to Adolf Hitler, the delegate from Europe.

Adolf stood beside Bernie, facing the demon congress. All stood and gave Adolf and Bernie a standing ovation that lasted five minutes.

Finally, Bernie left the stage and took his seat.

"This is a war for our survival," Adolf said. "If we lose, Satan loses his evil power, and God wins. There will be peace and goodwill on Earth for thousands of years.

"We know that archangels are the messengers from God, and they are immortal. Since we can't kill them or baby Jesus, we have to terrorize His believers by killing all the good people on Earth with bombs and shootings at any venue where believers attend.

"Four terrorist attacks I ordered to prepare will commence in an hour. The first will be on September tenth at 10:05 PM in Las Vegas, Nevada, at the Harvest Music Festival, a country and western concert. One of our demons, Stephen Paddock, will kill and maim as many concert goers as he can.

"Most of those who follow country and western music are law-abiding citizens who are believers. We have shooters in place with high-powered automatic weapons to kill and injure as many concert goers as we can. We will leave a note behind warning the survivors not to follow baby Jesus, or the same fate will befall them, too. This is our opening volley in the war to stop God's plan for peace on Earth.

"The second terrorist attack takes place in twelve hours when the Asian stock markets open. We have demon <u>cyber attackers</u> who will target worldwide computer infrastructure in an attempt to close down the system and create chaos. The same warning will be left on all the attacked computers. Image what people will do when they wake up and find they have no electricity and can't obtain money from their banks.

"The third terrorist attack will be at the World Trade Center in New York City at 8:46 AM on the morning of September eleven. I assigned a group of demons from the Middle East to highjack commercial airlines full of passengers and fly them into the World Trade Center buildings so hard the buildings will fall within minutes. There are over 100,000 workers in those buildings.

"We'll blame the attack on the Muslims, which will divide the world and have most Muslims come to our side without knowing it. We'll dupe them easily. The beauty of the plan is that it will fool the Western world into thinking Muslims performed such a horrific act. We'll gain one-third of the world's population to fight on our side and will use their belief that the enemy of my enemy is my friend. It's a win-win for Satan!"

The Fourth is a doozy! We have a demon dictator who will invade a peace loving, God following Eastern Europe country. The war will bomb schools and kill thousands very young children. Our demon dictator will bomb and destroy major cities. Thousands and thousands of innocent Gods loving people will be killed! Which will make living in the cities unlivable. The war will cause a major economic collapse in the whole world. Inflations will be out of control. The prices of fuels and food will go through the roof. This will cause an outrage and bring the free world to its knees.

There were cheers and loud applause. Satan stood and waved, staring at his supporters, as the ovation lasted five minutes.

"Our plan is to recruit as many evil people as we can," Satan continued. "Most of the violent prisoners already follow us. We'll need a large army to follow me and attack those who are being held prisoner in those prisons. Once freed, those prisoners will do whatever we say.

"I declare war against the worldwide believers of the Lord. The war begins in two hours with our attack on the believers in Las Vegas' country and western concert. We must win this war to prevent paradise on Earth. Let the war begin!"

Chapter

THREE

War on the Believers

Two hours after the vote, at the country and western music festival in Las Vegas, thousands of live rounds were fired into the crowd from different directions around the concert. Hundreds of innocent people were killed or wounded. People around the world stared at their TV sets, watching the shocking terrorist attack live.

Anthony watched the horrifying event on TV with his family at his house in Staten Island, New York. All of them were shocked by the bloody scene.

He was a New York City policeman who'd been fired for misdeeds while he was an officer. His son was arrested and convicted of selling drugs from their home on Staten Island that killed many young people when they overdosed.

Anthony gave free samples to kids until they were addicted, then they were his customers for life. Very successful at the business, he became rich while still young, causing untold misery and pain to the young people and their families.

Anthony and his family did anything they could to annoy their neighbors. Their dogs barked all day and night. They damaged tires on parked cars in the neighborhood, particularly if anyone parked in front of their house. They felt those spaces belonged to them or their customers who came to buy drugs.

Anthony beat his evil wife for not following orders outside the home and let the neighbors see him do it. His son sold drugs in front of the house.

Cars arrived at any time of the day or night so people could purchase drugs. Sometimes Anthony's son had drug and sex parties with underage girls in the cars parked in front of the house.

Neighbors complained to the police department, but nothing was done. It seemed Anthony and his family had a license to sell drugs from their home. He retained his contacts in the police department, who deliberately lost or destroyed all complaints against him. Finally, after many years of complaints piling up, the DEA arrested Anthony's son for drug dealing.

Anthony and his evil followers soon came to the attention of Satan and his demons. Satan sent his top lieutenant, Mike Dixon, to recruit Anthony and his family into the ranks of demons. Mike called and made an appointment to meet with Anthony at his home.

When Mike arrived, a loud barking dog greeted him. Anthony met him at the door and invited him inside to meet his wife, Eileen, and his son, Sal. Escorting him to their sun deck, they offered him a drink and lunch.

"Sure," Mike said. "What do you have?"

"Meatballs and spaghetti with the best homemade red sauce on Staten Island, made by Eileen. We also have expensive red wine that is usually served only at the finest Manhattan restaurants."

"You just made my day. With lunch, can you get me six oxycodone pills to go with the wine? That'll be dessert."

They laughed.

"Sure," Anthony said.

They began their conversation over the constantly barking family dog. Mike explained he benefits of joining Satan's demon army. They amounted to more money than a Congressman made. To sweeten the deal, Satan promised to watch over Anthony's son in prison. Mike added that if Anthony refused the deal, the son in prison would be harmed.

"Take it or leave it," Mike said. "You have thirty minutes."

Anthony was taken aback by the offer and threat. "Look, Mike, things are going well for me and my family. I don't need money. We're already rich. I need time to think over a big decision like this."

"Satan gave you thirty minutes to decide. You have twenty-eight minutes left. He has an assignment for you at the World Trade Center this Tuesday, the eleventh. You have to decide today. Remember, your son's life is in danger in prison if you don't go along."

Eileen arrived with lunch, wine, and the six oxycodone pills. Mike put the pills into his mouth and swallowed them. Within minutes, the drug took effect, making him more demanding than before.

"Stan will show you how much power he has," Mike warned. "Your son in prison is in terrible danger. I can guarantee he'll do whatever Satan wants. After you find out what happened to him, I'm sure you'll agree to our terms and conditions."

He handed a list to Anthony. "You'll bring a laundry bag of fraudulent votes from dead people to the election polls at Egbert Junior High School. Deliver them to Demon Bruce in the parking lot at seven o'clock in the morning on Tuesday, September eleventh.

"Then take the Staten Island Ferry to Manhattan and go to Versey Street to meet Demon Howard at 8:45 AM. You'd better not be late. In front of the telephone company, he'll give you a semiautomatic .306 rifle with bump stock and fifty clips of ammo. You'll station yourself facing the stairs were workers will try to flee the World Trade Center. When Demon Howard gives you the order to fire, you must shoot all the workers who try to escape."

"Can I ask why they'll be fleeing the building?"

"No. That's all the information you need. I promise you that if you don't join us now, it'll be too late to stop what's going to happen to your son in prison. That's how we recruit demon followers. Once something happens to a loved one, they beg to join us. You'll beg, too.

"We won't stop until you join. The next thing will be Eileen. It'll be much worse for her. Then, if you still refuse, you're next. What happened to your wife and son will seem like a vacation compared to what we'll do to you.

"I know you'll agree. As of now, your life and the lives of your family are in your hands. You have no choice but to join us. When you show up at the World Trade Center, Demon Howard will know that you've decided to join us."

"I won't join Satan under those terms. I'd have no life. I'd be his slave. Look, Demon Mike, thanks but no thanks. I don't believe Satan has that kind of power. I'll take my chances on enjoying life with my family."

"I'll leave this bag of fraudulent ballots in case you change your mind. When you decide to join us, bring the ballots to Demon Bruce at the polling place at seven in the morning, then meet Demon Howard at the World Trade Center at 8:45."

"You sure take a lot for granted. I already made my decision not to join."

"Still, I'll leave the ballots in case you do. Let's finish our lunch and wine and get to know each other. I have the feeling we'll be spending a lot of time together."

The family joined them for lunch, and the topic of joining Satan never arose again. Demon Mike suggested ways Anthony could increase his profit on selling drugs, and Anthony thanked him for his advice, adding he would try it.

After lunch, Demon Mike stood, and they all said good-bye. He turned to Anthony. "I know you'll be at the World Trade Center on the eleventh."

"Don't bet on it."

Demon Mike left.

Eileen turned to Anthony. "What was that about? What's in the large bag? I hope it's money."

"This was a waste of time. It was all BS. Mike sounds nuts. I didn't believe a word he said, so let's just drop it."

"I have to know what he said."

"He was spinning a tale and telling me wild stories. If I don't do what he says, bad things will happen to our son in jail. It's BS.

"He said this bag has fraudulent absentee ballots in it. I'm supposed to take them to the polling place. Let's check."

They walked to the large bag and opened it. Inside were piles of notarized absentee ballots.

"There must be thousands in here," Anthony said. "It looks like enough to change the results of the election."

"Do you still think it's BS? I'm worried."

"Let's wait and see. If I join Satan, we won't have a happy life together. We'll be Satan's slaves. That's a lot to ask."

"I hope you're right, but I'm worried about our son in jail. Let's see what happens."

Anthony's phone rang at 4:30 AM on September 11.

"Who would call at such an ungodly hour?" he grumbled, reaching for the receiver. "Hello?"

"This is <u>Fran,</u> the registered nurse at Sing Sing Prison ICU. Your son had been gang raped in the exercise yard by at least twelve prisoners. He's in a coma. I've never seen such severe injuries before. It almost looks like it was done by devil worshippers.

"Your son has a less than fifty-fifty chance of survival. Since this is a prison, you can't visit the hospital ward without a court order. I'll call if there's any change in his condition.

"There was one strange thing. Prison investigators found a note in his pants pocket that read, *Anthony go to the assigned location and meet Howard, or your wife is next.* Are you the Anthony who's being referred to?"

"Holy shit! Satan is right!" He immediately regained his composure. "No, I'm not the Anthony that note is for. I don't know anyone named Howard or what assignment it means. I'll go to court to get a pass so I can see my son. Is there anything I can do for him at this point?"

"Pray to God. We have doctors with plenty of experience. They'll do the best they can for your son."

Anthony hung up and turned to Eileen, who was awake and overheard the conversation. "I have no choice. I have to do what Satan wants. I'll wash and dress, then I'll take the fraudulent ballots to Bruce at the polling site. After that, I have to go to the World Trade Center and meet Howard. I have to do whatever I can to save you and our son.

"I can see how Satan recruits people. He blackmails them. I can only imagine what he'll do to us once we become members of the demon army, but we have no choice. If I don't do what Satan wants, you're the next victim. Maybe, if I do what Satan asks, I can save our son."

"Satan is a piece of shit. How can we follow such a bastard? We have to save our son. Can we get away once we join Satan's followers? I don't know if we can. If not, we're screwed, but our lives are ruined, anyway.

"Now I know how families feel when they lose children to drug overdoses. Go do what you must, Anthony."

He left the house in his most-comfortable clothes and sneakers, assuming he would do a lot of running after he shot at the people fleeing the World Trade Center.

He arrived at Egbert Junior High School and met Demon Bruce on time in the parking lot.

"Are you Bruce, the person I'm supposed to meet?" he asked nervously.

"Yes, Anthony. Satan's representative texted me a picture of you. I know about you, your son, and your wife and the situation you're in. Let's get down to business. I'm your supervisor now, and you follow my orders. Got it? If I tell Demon Mike you didn't listen to me, you and your family are finished. Pay attention."

Terrified, Anthony stood at attention, staring into Demon Bruce's eyes.

"That's better. I believe you got the message that Satan is in charge, and you have to do whatever he and his lieutenant order you to do. Where's the laundry bag of fraudulent ballots?"

"In the trunk of my car."

"At ease."

They walked to the car and opened the trunk. Anthony opened the bag, and Demon Bruce grabbed some of the fraudulent ballots to examine until he was satisfied they had enough to change the final count for the New York City board of elections.

"You'll find out that Satan holds all his followers responsible for their assignments," he told Anthony. "If anything goes wrong, even if it's your first mistake, he'll make an example of you in front of the demon congress.

"He's got a big cage that sits on a fire pit. He puts wrongdoers in there, locks the door, and unties the person so he's free to run. A fire is set under the cage. The demons watch, as the prisoner dies a slow, agonizing death. Satan doesn't forgive if an order isn't fulfilled."

Anthony wondered what he'd gotten himself and his family into. He knew he wasn't perfect and would make a mistake somewhere, which meant he would be burned alive someday. He decided to go through the motions and leave the organization as soon as possible.

"What do you want me to do?" Anthony asked.

"Go into the polling place and register to vote as Demon Deadman John P. Last. Go to voting booth number six and hold down the tab for Demon Candidate William Garnett for three minutes. The machine is rigged to tally enough votes to make him win the election.

"Satan wants him to win. He's been a devoted follower since he got into office. He caused countless families a lot of pain and suffering with the laws he passed.

"Don't acknowledge me when you see me at the table in the polling site. I'll deliberately give you a hard time. I'll ask for your driver's license, so just open your wallet and show it. I'll look at it but don't care if it's a driver's license. You'll pass as John P. Last, a dead voter. I'll let you in to vote. Got it?

"After you vote 1,956 times for Garnett, I want you to leave and take the Staten Island Ferry at seven-thirty. When you arrive at the Battery in Lower Manhattan, you have to walk up Broadway to Vesey Street, where you'll meet Demon Howard in front of the phone company at eight forty-five. He'll give you the weapons you need and the ammo. You follow whatever orders he gives you. Got that?"

"Yes, Sir!"

"Dismissed. Get in there and vote."

Anthony went inside and followed orders.

As Anthony drove to the Staten Island train station, he thought about the mess he got his family into. Whatever he did, he couldn't win. He became so angry that he actually looked forward to killing the innocence people who left the World Trade Tower.

He parked his new Mercedes Benz with only 900 miles on it at the Annadale Station parking lot and wondered if he'd ever see the car again. The station was crowded with commuters and students. September 11 was a beautiful day, with a clear, blue sky and temperatures in the seventies.

He stood against the wall of the train station, waiting for the train, when a distinguished man in his forties in a nice business suit came over with a very stern expression.

"Do you remember me?" the man asked.

Looking puzzled, Anthony said, "No."

"I'm Bob. You might remember my wife, Josephine. We were the parents of Jennifer, a young, beautiful girl your son killed by selling her drugs. We testified at the trial for your piece-of-shit son. I hoped and prayed that someday I'd meet you and tell you what I think of you and your family. You're nothing but scum, and I wish you and all your family a painful, slow death. I have a gift for you, too. I hoped our paths would cross someday."

Anthony, taken aback by the vehemence in the man's tone, shoved Bob away with both hands. He punched Bob's stomach. As Bob fell, he hit his head hard on the concrete floor, then drew his licensed .38 and shot Anthony in the shoulder once before missing with the next four bullets.

Anthony didn't dare stay and report the incident to the police. He had to meet Demon Howard at 8:45 AM at the World Trade Center. Although he was in excruciating pain in his left shoulder, he ran to his car in the parking lot, opened the door, and grabbed a rag that he used to clean the windows. Pressing it against the wound to stop the bleeding, he drove toward the World Trade Center at high speed.

Running red lights, he passed many cars. To his surprise, the police didn't stop him, although he broke most of the traffic laws on his way.

He is reaching the World Trade Center still bleeding profusely. Blood covered his seat. The ruined car would need a completely new interior.

Anthony needed to find a bathroom. He double-parked on Broadway, not caring if anyone towed the car. He doubted he'd see it again, anyway.

Running into the building, he stopped at the security desk. One of the guards recognized him from his days at the New York City Police Department when they shared a patrol car.

Pete looked at him and asked, "What happened to you?"

"It's a long story, but I need a bathroom to take care of my injury. Where is it?"

"I'll escort you. There's a medical department on the eighty-second floor. Do you want me to take you up there? I'm good friends with the doctors and think I can get you in right away."

Anthony glanced at his watch only to realize it stopped after his fight with Bob, showing 7:35 AM. The pain was so severe, he realized he had to see a doctor. He couldn't fulfill the mission for Satan and wouldn't be able to aim the gun without some kind of padding or a bandage.

He decided to tell the doctor he'd been shot while driving to work, and he had to leave at 8:30 to meet someone at Vesey Street four blocks away.

Pete escorted Anthony to the elevator, which was crowded with people going to work. It was already 8:46 AM, although Anthony didn't know it.

"What time is it?" he asked Pete.

Pete glanced at his watch. "Eight forty-six."

Shocked, Anthony realized he and his family would die from horrible deaths at Satan's hands, because he missed his appointment with Demon Howard.

Just as Anthony opened his mouth to speak, there was a large explosion. The building swayed. Passengers screamed and pushed against each other. The elevator screeched to a halt, and the lights flickered and died.

Everyone in the elevator car panicked, screaming and trying to get out. They were trapped in the dark with no fresh air to breathe.

Anthony knew he and all the others would die an excruciating death at Satan's hands.

Cell phones in the elevator rang, and passengers answered in panicky voices. They soon learned that a plane struck the building at the 82nd floor. All cell phones died, and more panic erupted.

"First the shooting in Las Vegas, now this!" someone said. "The devil must be involved in these attacks."

After five minutes in the pitch-black elevator, they smelled smoke and began choking and coughing. Fiery debris from above struck the roof of the car with loud bangs, making people shriek in alarm. All of them knew they were doomed. Some started praying to God.

At 9:59 AM, the elevator car collapsed when American Airlines flight 11 struck the building. All the people in the elevator car died. No one knew what happened to Anthony and the passengers. Their bodies became dust among the rubble of the collapsed building.

Chapter FOUR

Satan, Party Time

Satan called the demon congress to order. "We've had a wonderful couple of days. We caused misery and death to thousands of good people around the world. The believers are on the run. They will surrender within days."

He signaled Adolf Hitler to approach the podium to give them an update.

Demon Hitler stood on the podium and faced the congress. "We've been very successful in the past two days with our terrorist attacks in Las Vegas, some school shootings, and the attack on the World Trade Center. We killed and injured thousands of innocent believers at minimal cost. It was less than $5,000 for all these attacks.

"We have the entire Western world blaming the Muslims for all the terrorist attacks around the world. If Satan agrees to our plan, we can win our war against the believers in seven days. Our strategy will be to divide and conquer the Western world, the Middle East, and Russia. We'll drag Russia, a nuclear power, into the Muslim side of the war.

"We already confiscated four nuclear submarines. We have demon crews in command of them, waiting to fire their missiles on Satan's order at any target we choose. Two submarines came from Russia, and two came from America. Both countries will believe that the other started World War Three. The beauty is, it will cost Satan almost nothing to start and win the war against the believers.

"We can start the war in five days. Once it is over, the free world where the believers live will be destroyed. Satan will rule the world and can enslave any believers still alive."

The demon congress gave Hitler a standing ovation.

Satan slowly stood from his seat in the center of the table and stared down at the congress. "I have declared war on the believers. There will be no vote. I accept Hitler's plan for World War Three. It begins in five days. I am also proclaiming marshal law and will suspend all voting in this congress. All decisions for running the war will come from me.

"Now for new business. When I call the following demon names, they will come to the front of the stage where I can give them special awards."

He checked his list. "The Demon Senators from Italy, Sal and Marie; the Demon Senator for Canada, Max."

Demon Jenifer and her live-in boyfriend Tony, along with Dick, Blake, Frank Averill, and his family, sat in the audience from the U.S.

The demon senators stood and walked to the front, where they turned to face the demon assembly with smiles.

Satan began reading a proclamation, and the more he said, the more obvious it became that he wasn't giving an award. He was pronouncing death sentences for the ones he called.

He charged and convicted them for high crimes and misdemeanors. Their sentence was death.

"We're at war," Satan announced. "We can't tolerate any acts of desertion in the fulfillment of our mission to rule the world and enslave the believers. Handcuff them and escort them to the cage."

The Senators resisted, but the guard subdued them. The prisoners screamed and shouted they were innocent of all charges, but the guards ignored that and dragged them to the cage door before shoving them inside.

"I have a bonus for you!" Satan announced. He signaled other guards to bring the families of the caged Senators to the front.

Soon, all thirty of the Senators' wives and husbands, children and pets, were placed in the cage with the Senators.

Satan checked the people and saw someone was missing. "Where are Bob Cromwell and his new wife, Bonnie? Bring him to me right now! He is the ex-husband of Demon Judy Cromwell. Send a squad of demon guards to locate him in Canada. I'll spare no expense to find him. I'll give a reward of $250,000 Canadian dollars to anyone who captures them!"

A squad of twenty demon guards immediately left for Canada.

The assembled family members, realizing they, too, would be locked in the cage, tried to run. Guards caught and subdued them, dragging them to the cage door and placing them inside. The people inside began screaming, proclaiming their innocence.

A hush fell, as Satan signaled his guard commander. The fire was lit at one end under the cage, making the prisoners run to the far side to escape the flames. They were closest to the demon congress, letting them have a good view of their torture and death.

The fire slowly spread toward the middle of the cage. Half of the cage became a raging inferno. The more the prisoners panicked and cried out for help, the more the demon congress applauded and cheered, watching the fire move closer to the terrified prisoners. The prisoners did everything they could to escape, pushing, kicking, and trampling the other prisoners.

The place where Demon Jenifer died started a new fire in the pit near the other prisoners. They climbed over each other in their panic to escape their fate.

After twenty minutes, the entire cage was ablaze. The people caught fire, too, and the odor of burning flesh filled the congress. Prisoners shouted in pain, then slowly fell silent.

The execution ended thirty minutes later, and the Senators gave Satan a standing ovation.

Guards hosed down the cage with water. Once the cage was cool enough, eight horses were harnessed to one end to pull the cage to its storage site where it could be cleaned and prepared for its next use.

"All of you will soon receive my orders on what is required to win this war and enslave the believers," Satan told them. "Let the war begin! This congress is dismissed."

Every twenty minutes, the TV news showed another terrorist attack somewhere in the world. Announcements interrupted all shows on all channels, listing the increasing number of children and religious leaders who were killed.

The good believers began to panic. Stores ran out of food and soon had empty shelves. Long lines of people stood outside, demanding to be allowed in to buy what they needed for their families. Gas stations quickly ran out of gasoline. Riots and looting began in all large cities worldwide.

At noon on the first day of Satan's war against the believers, all TV and radio stations suddenly switched to Satan and his demon congress, showing a disheveled Satan standing at his podium to address the world's people.

He stared into the camera and said, "To all the believers in the world. You will obey me and follow my orders, or you and your loved ones will face horrible deaths. We know God sent baby Jesus to Earth a second time to create peace and rid the planet of demons. I and my demon followers will stop Him from achieving that goal. I declare war on all believers in the world!"

The TV and radio stations showed the demon congress, where the members stood to cheer and applaud. Adolf Hitler gave the Nazi salute, then the cameras returned to Satan.

"I order my new and old followers to kill as many good people in the world as possible over the next seven days," Satan continued. "We will have total victory within that time. Believers must submit and join us or die.

"I order you to stay away from your houses of worship. That will show you're a believer, and we will target you and your family for death. Let the war begin!"

All TV and radio stations went off the air.

Within minutes, gunfire echoed down the streets of all major cities in the world, as hundreds, then thousands, of good people were murdered in the streets. Fires started in large buildings. Emergency sirens screamed, as vehicles rushed to the streets, trying to save people.

The countries that had strict gun control laws couldn't defend their citizens and were at the mercy of the demons, who raped and killed thousands of defenseless good people. All essential supplies ran out. The world descended into chaos.

Chapter

FIVE

Panicked World Leaders Call for Emergency UN Meeting

Mary, Joseph, and Jesus were in their apartment on Coney Island, Brooklyn, watching Satan on TV, when suddenly, Mary and Joseph fell into a deep sleep and began to dream, hearing God speak to them.

"You will be contacted by the United Nations to address all the world delegates," God said in a soft, gentle voice. "You will speak to the world while holding baby Jesus in your arms. He will tell you what to say to the delegates about how to achieve paradise on Earth.

"We will defeat Satan and his followers in seven days. When you both wake up, answer the phone. It will be a call from the President. He will ask you to address the United Nations. Accept the invitation. You must tell the world that all good people must attend their houses of worship regularly and become believers in God.

"All good people and their families will be saved and will live the remainder of their lives free from evil, prejudice, and war. There will be paradise on Earth. All the good people of the world will be with you and will support you and baby Jesus."

Mary and Joseph, slowly making the sign of the cross on their chests, thanked God for choosing them to save the world with baby Jesus.

They woke to hear the phone ringing. Mary carried the baby in her arms, as she ran to answer. "Hello?"

"Mary, how are you and baby Jesus doing?" the President asked. "I hope you're well. We face a national emergency, and the world needs you, baby Jesus, and God's help to stop Satan and his demons in this war.

"I had a dream that I spoke to God and was told to call to invite you, Joseph, and baby Jesus to address the delegates at the United Nations. We need a plan to achieve victory in the war against Satan. Will you come?"

"God has a plan to rid Earth of Satan and his demons," Mary said confidently. "Our world will become a paradise. He will communicate with all the UN delegates a way to achieve victory over Satan and his demons. The meeting of the general assembly must be held Thursday at nine o'clock in the morning. That is God's will.

"The believers will be victorious in the war against Satan and his followers in seven days. I can't emphasize enough that all good people and believers must attend their houses of worship this weekend to avoid being classified as demons. Tell the good people of the world that God will speak to them in their houses or worship this weekend.

"God has chosen a church in St. Petersburg, Florida, as His headquarters. It's a small building on the corner of 38th Avenue that was built in 1958. That's all I know about it. Good people and believers can search the Internet to locate it. They will be blessed by God.

"Mr. President, God wants you to sign an executive order declaring a state of national emergency and calling for marshal law right after the UN meeting. God knows we will have a successful vote to defeat Satan. He wants you to call Congress to an emergency session to implement all the resources America can muster to implement His plan."

"If there is anything else God wants us to do, please call my private phone line." The President gave her the number.

"Thank you, Mr. President."

They ended the call.

Mary held baby Jesus in her arms and turned to face the cameras people held in the room. "To all the good people and believers in the world—go to your houses of worship this weekend and wait for instructions from God to rid our wonderful world of Satan and his demon followers.

"You and your family will be safe if you believe in God and follow His teaching. Live your lives in peace and tolerance and attend worship services each week. If you don't, you'll be treated like the demons."

Bob Cromwell laid on the couch, watching TV in the living room, after a workout in the gym at his house. Falling into a deep sleep, he dreamed he saw God in a beautiful garden with a waterfall and peaceful scenery all around.

"Bob," God said in a soft, reassuring voice, "I'm giving you and Bonnie a warning. Satan has sent twenty demons to arrest you both. They'll bring you to the demon congress to torture you by putting you in a cage with other demons to be set on fire and burned alive.

"If you and Bonnie promise to attend your house of worship and believe in Me, I'll give you a plan to spare you both. You'll live the rest of your lives in paradise on Earth. Will you promise to become a believer?"

Bob went to his knees and made the sign of the cross. "I promise You, God, that Bonnie and I will go to church and become believers. We will follow You with our hearts and souls."

He gave Bob a telephone number. "That is the number of Captain Mary Ellen, the commander of the demon squad that's coming to arrest you. Call this number at noon today your time, and tell Captain Mary Ellen to meet you and Bonnie at Reversing Falls by the bridge in St. John, Canada, today at three o'clock.

"All twenty demon guards will be there. You and Bonnie will stand in the middle of the bridge with Archangel John Daniels to guide you about what to do to deal with those guards. As long as you follow the archangel's orders, you and Bonnie will be safe. I placed cameras on the bridge to live stream the arrest attempt. The whole world will be watching to see the power of God achieve peace and win the war against Satan.

"The demons will order you and Bonnie to surrender. Believe in Me, your God, and I promise that you and Bonnie won't be harmed when you surrender in peace."

"Will we be tortured after we surrender? Is there any way to fight the demons? We don't have access to guns in Canada, so how can we defend ourselves?"

"I promise you won't be harmed. I'll show you the power of God to do good. Let the demon squad meet you two at the middle of the bridge, and I will do the rest."

Bob awoke from his sleep and remembered it was Wednesday. A glance at his watch showed it was 11:55 AM. In a panic, he looked for his cell phone to call the demon commander and make the appointment to meet him at the bridge.

At exactly noon, he called the number God gave him. It rang once, then Captain Mary Ellen answered.

"Who's calling, and what do you want?" she demanded.

"This is Bob Cromwell. I heard Satan wants to talk to me and Bonnie. We aren't looking for a fight. We'll surrender to you peacefully. Let's meet at Reversing Falls in St. John, Canada at three o'clock this afternoon. Is that OK with you?"

"Just in case you try to pull a fast one, I want to meet in the middle of the bridge. You and Bonnie will stand with your hands up and face the falls. Both of you have to wear tight shorts and tight T-shirts and flip-flops. All your pants pockets must be turned out. If either of you tries something, we'll kill you. Got that? Don't bring anyone with you. You must come alone."

"We're at Satan's mercy. We'll do as you say. God bless you."

"There is no god but Satan! We'll see you in hell."

Bob and Bonnie parked their car at the foot of the bridge overlooking Reverse Falls at 2:30 PM. They looked at each other.

"I think we're in over our heads," Bob said, "confronting Satan's followers like this. We must put our faith in God's hands, along with Archangel John Daniels. We'll be all right.

"Let's show them we have total faith in God. We should leave out the crucifix on its chain around our necks, so they can see them resting on top of our T-shirts. That should tick them off."

They pulled out the gold crucifixes they wore and let them hang.

At 2:59 PM, they stood on the highest point in the middle of the bridge, waiting for the demons to arrive. They wondered where the archangel was.

Looking up at the clouds in the sky, they didn't notice that some of them were dark gold, forming an image of God.

Bob checked his watch and saw it was 3:00. He turned left and saw soldiers marching up the bridge toward them. He turned to Bonnie, hugged her, and then they prayed.

"Halt!" Captain Mary Ellen said when the guards were twenty yards from the couple. "Take positions!"

The guards formed two ranks, with ten down on one knee, while the other ten stood up, all aiming their rifles at Bob and Bonnie.

Captain Mary Ellen stepped forward. "Step away from each other and face us. Turn your pockets inside out, turn slowly, and raise your hands above your heads."

They complied with the orders. Captain Mary Ellen walked over and took two pair of handcuffs from her belt. "Turn around, infidel, and put your hands behind your back." She grabbed the crucifix hanging around Bob's neck and tossed it over the bridge, as Bob finished turning around.

Suddenly, a bright light lit up the sky. Everyone looked up and saw the sky parting above them. Bright lightning bolts blinded them, followed by a deafening crash of thunder.

Bob and Bonnie saw the demon soldiers shaking and dropping their weapons. Some, breaking ranks, looked for places to hide. Most of them huddled together and began crying. A few shouted, "Forgive me, God!"

"Get back in ranks!" Captain Mary Ellen shouted.

None of the demons moved.

A bolt of lightning struck the bridge a few feet from her, knocking her down and setting her uniform on fire. Bob and Bonnie were unharmed. They grabbed the woman and put out the fire.

A large, bright white puff of smoke appeared where the lightning struck the bridge, and Archangel John Daniel walked out of the haze. He faced the cameras on the bridge and said, "I'm a messenger from God. Baby Jesus has been sent to Earth to rid the world of its demons and create peace, tolerance, and prosperity for the New Jerusalem. Any demon or nonbeliever who doesn't become a true believer in God will suffer a mental breakdown. The pain and suffering will be so intense, they will have only three options—they can commit suicide, be transported to hell, or become a believer. That is the fate for anyone who confuses God and Satan."

He motioned to the cameras, then he walked to Captain Mary Ellen, whose face showed pain from the fire, as smoke rose from her burned body. When he touched her head, she looked up, and the pain transformed into a smile. She fell into a deep sleep, twisting and turning while muttering and screaming.

Bob and Bonnie saw the twenty soldiers were also on the ground, writhing and screaming in a deep sleep.

After twenty-seven minutes, Captain Mary Ellen woke and looked up at the archangel standing over her. She faced the cameras and said in a soft voice, "I spoke to my God, and I instantly became a believer in His word. I will go to my house of worship this Sunday as God wants us to do, to hear His words and learn how to achieve peace on Earth. I beg all the demons of the world to leave Satan, who is totally evil. They must believe in God, who is totally good, to save them from evil."

She touched herself and found all her pain was gone. Looking up at the clouds that still formed God's image, she said, "Thank You, God," and stood up.

Looking at her squad of soldiers, she saw only two were still in deep sleep. She walked over and shook one of them called Rocky. When he awoke, he was screaming and cursing God.

She tried to calm him without success. Rocky stood, still screaming, and raced in circles.

"He's out of control," she said.

Bob and Bonnie grabbed the soldier and held him down. He looked up at the sky and cursed God.

"I am and will die a Satan demon!" he shouted. "I know God is most powerful and will win this war, because good is with Him. Satan is evil and will be doomed forever, but I'm too confused to know who to follow. I can't think straight."

Breaking free, he ran toward the rail of the bridge, then looked back at the archangel, Bob, Bonnie, and the other demon soldiers. "If you don't believe in your God, you go crazy. Then your only choice is to commit suicide."

He turned toward the rail, cursed God one last time, and jumped to his death.

Everyone ran to the rail and looked down, but Rocky's body wasn't visible in the St. John River.

Archangel John Daniel faced the cameras. "All believers can live in peace on Earth if you follow God's message. If you don't, you'll share the same fate as Demon Rocky—you'll go mad and have to commit excruciating suicide. That's the choice for nonbelievers."

Demon Sam got up and ran around the bridge next, cursing God and flailing his arms against his head. From what the others could understand, he apparently decided to follow Satan, not God.

He took out his machete and began stabbing himself in the stomach. He fell down on his back, screaming in pain. Raising, the machete, he stabbed himself in the eye before rolling over and gasping, "I will follow Satan! Damn God!" He slit his throat so hard, his head almost separated from the body.

People who lived in St. John's and watched the live stream converged on the bridge to see if Archangel John Daniel, Bob, or Bonnie needed any assistance with the demon soldiers.

The crowd rushed forward and halted 100 yards from the center of the bridge.

"Believe in your God," Archangel John Daniel said softly. "Follow Him. Baby Jesus is the messenger for God on Earth. He has come for the second time to save Earth from Satan. Listen to Him and follow His words.

"All believers in the world will have enough food and water to last one day, until Thursday night. At midnight on Thursday, the second coming of Passover will begin, lasting until sunrise on Saturday. People must remain in their homes for eight hours, where they will speak with God. Lock yourselves in and secure your homes for the night of Passover.

"All good believers living in the city of New York and the surrounding area must leave their places of residence by 8:45 AM on Thursday morning. That is a direct order from God. The twenty-mile area must be secure for all world leaders to attend an emergency meeting at the United Nations.

"God has ordered no religious leaders or the aides will be permitted to this emergency meeting. Only world leaders and their aides are allowed in. Police officers and security personnel will also leave Manhattan and take up positions on the twenty-mile radius surrounding the city. That is God's will.

"At that time, all people in the world will decide if they wish to believe in God or Satan. Believers will live in paradise on Earth and have a wonderful life of peace, tolerance, and prosperity in the New Jerusalem.

"Those who don't follow God will go instantly insane and suffer horrible death by suicide or be transported to hell to suffer eternally. It is up to you."

He motioned Bob and Bonnie to come forward and kneel. "I will install you two as ambassadors to God on Earth to assist baby Jesus and Mary in their work. Help them achieve paradise on Earth. When you enter paradise yourself, you will be eligible to be angels in paradise if you fulfill good lives as believers."

Bob and Bonnie nodded. The archangel performed the ceremony in front of the crowd and the watching cameras. Cheers and loud applause came from the crowd at the foot of the bridge.

When the ceremony ended, Archangel John Daniel said good-bye to the people on the bridge and the Internet. Lightning struck in front of him, creating a large puff of smoke that rose until it touched a beautiful white cloud hovering in the sky.

When the smoke dissipated, the archangel was gone.

Chapter

SIX

United Nations

Every world leader received notice to attend the emergency meeting at 9:00 AM Thursday to make plans to eliminate Satan and his followers from the world.

All the airports and Air Force bases around New York City were busy with planes landing and taking off every few seconds. All the world leaders had to be in the United Nations building by 8:00, because the airports were due to close at 7:15.

VIP motorcades clogged the highways and streets, with New York City police escorting them with sirens and lights. All believers living in the twenty-mile area left and found other places to stay.

Over one million nonbelievers elected to stay behind, unwilling to follow God's order.

No hotel rooms were available for all the dignitaries who arrived. They made the best of the situation by sleeping in their embassies, in churches, and at police stations. Some even slept in their rented cars. All of them tried to get a good night's sleep, so they could attend the most-important meeting ever held at the UN.

At exactly 9:00 AM, the meeting was called to order. On the stage facing the crowded hall was the Secretary General of the UN, with the United States President at his right side. World leaders filled up the remaining space on the stage and occupied the open area before it. Some even sat on the floor, while others stood behind them or sat at desks. Every available inch of space was occupied. Those who didn't find room in the assembly hall stood in offices throughout the building. They would use their cell phones to communicate with the Secretary General through aides who would relay the questions to the stage.

The Secretary General stood in front of the assembly and banged his gavel, calling the emergency meeting to order. He had to bang it twelve times before silence fell.

"I would like to introduce the President of the United States," the Secretary General said. "First, I want all of us here in this building and anyone watching via TV to stand and pray to God."

When the prayer ended, he said, "Baby Jesus and Mary will join us after we decide how to defeat Satan and his demons. After we vote on how to wage that war, baby Jesus will have God speak to all world leaders. Please don't leave the meeting after the vote.

"We know that some world leaders are egotistical, self-serving, and corrupt and don't care at all for the people they are supposed to serve. All of us must put that aside and do good for mankind. It might feel as difficult as talking to a wall to persuade some leaders to become believers, but we must give everyone that choice.

"Most of us know who the leaders are who don't care about their fellow man. We must put our feelings aside and do the right thing to achieve world peace."

Looking at the packed audience, he saw that over 80% of the leaders were getting up from their seats and leading their entourages toward the exits after such a brow-beating. The Secretary General feared the emergency meeting would end in total failure, with no way to stop Satan.

Just at 9:15, a bright flash of light blinded everyone in the room. A loud bang sounded, knocking them down, as the ceiling and walls shook and collapsed, burying the assembled people. The smoke and heat intensified until the furniture burst into flame or melted. Paint bubbled off from the intense heat, then a fire quickly engulfed the entire building.

In a fraction of a second, everyone in the United Nations assembly died and turned to dust, as the building went up in fire. All of Manhattan burned with it, disappearing into dust and clouds that rose in four mushroom clouds.

New York City was gone. Everything within the twenty-mile radius was vaporized in the nuclear bomb attack led by Satan's followers in two submarines.

Baby Jesus, Mary, and Joseph were safe in Franklin Lakes, New Jersey, in the home of Archangel Alma Robbin's relatives. It was far from New York City and was downwind from the nuclear attack that destroyed the city. All electric, water, and communications facilities went down on the entire East Coast.

People around the world witnessed the nuclear attack on the Internet and began to panic. Riots, looting, and mass shootings began, as Satan's minions killed believers in cities around the world. Satan and his demons knew they just won the battle against God. He ordered his demons to increase their attacks. Soon, he received reports that tens of thousands of believers were dead, and total chaos reigned in most major cities around the world.

He called the demon congress to order. "We're winning the war against God's people in the world. Our plan is working. We'll finish this war within seven days."

The congress gave him a standing ovation that lasted seven minutes. Finally, he banged the gavel to call the room to order again.

"All the world leaders died in our attack using nuclear bombs," Satan continued. "I sacrificed many of our own demonic world leaders, but they died to allow us the chance to cause chaos in the world. We will honor the fallen leaders with portraits that will hang on the walls of this congress, honoring them for their sacrifice.

"If anyone is still thinking about the incident on the bridge in Canada, where eighteen of our soldiers surrendered and became believers, that was just a fluke. We can train our demons how to prevent that from happening again."

He didn't let anyone know that was a lie. He had no idea how to stop God from converting demons into believers. If Satan didn't come up with something, he knew God and his believers would win the war.

TV cameras in the hall brought Satan's words to demons watching from around the world.

"I have all my top believers working on ways to prevent God from converting any more demons to His side. One idea is to invade the houses of worship, where God can't put nonbelievers to sleep and convert them. We will occupy all the places of worship in the world. That is being done as I speak. We must be in charge of all churches, synagogues, and temples by three o'clock this afternoon, before Passover begins.

"Our demon soldiers have already overrun the Vatican and taken the city. The artwork we now possess is priceless and will be worth enough to repair any damage done to the world in this war.

"No demon should sleep until he visits the Vatican or some other place of worship. Stay put and take the pills we have issued every four hours for the next twelve hours. The pills have been distributed to your desks, along with food. Leave the demon congress as soon as possible, pack your bags for a week, and then we will defeat god!

"Our next meeting will be at nine o'clock tomorrow at the Vatican in Rome, Italy, which will be televised. We'll be safe in God's houses of worship!"

Cheers and applause came from the demon congressmen. Satan paused to ask if Adolf Hitler wanted to address the congress.

He came to the stage with his war strategist, Dana, his right-hand person who helped plan the successful attack against the United Nations building.

"We've had a great two days in our fight against God," Hitler said. "We have killed and maimed millions of believers. We have wiped out almost all world leaders. There is no one left to take charge of the believers' governments. They're leaderless and totally bewildered."

He turned to Dana, who stepped up to the front of the podium and said, "Our demon followers are creating chaos in the world against all believers. We've been very successful in all our battles. Our war plan is on schedule. Satan will win the war against God in the next five days! They remaining believers don't have any government leaders left to follow, and they are adrift and bewildered. By using all the nuclear weapons we had on hand, we killed the world leaders and destroyed New York City!"

Satan suddenly shouted, "You used all our nuclear missiles from both submarines on the UN building? That's crazy! We could have used a few of them on other cities in the world to win this war."

"Killing the world leaders was the most-important mission in winning the war against the believers," Dana said.

Satan grew increasingly angry. "Using up all our missiles in one battle was a big mistake. It'll take weeks to place demons in control of other nuclear weapons!"

He stood and shouted, "Arrest Demon Dana and bring out the cage!"

Six guards grabbed her and kicked and punched her down to the floor, where she was subdued and handcuffed.

The cage rolled out and covered the fire pit. The door was opened, and Demon Dan was tossed inside. She hit her head against the cage wall and started bleeding profusely.

"Satan, why are you doing this to me?" she shouted. "I've been a devoted supporter and admirer of you! Please give me a second chance!"

He eyed her sternly. "I won't burn you alive."

"Thank you, Satan!"

A slow smile crept over Satan's face. "I'll hang you in the cage and carve you up. We'll serve pieces of you to the other demons for lunch."

"No! No!" she shrieked.

Ten guards retrieved the hangman's rope and wrapped it around the top of the cage, then lowered the end to place around Dana's neck. It was so tight, she had trouble breathing.

They waited for Satan's order to walk slowly with the rope over their shoulders, strangling Demon Dana to death.

"Lunch! Lunch! Lunch!" the congressmen shouted.

Satan raised his left hand over his head with his thumb up, then turned it down. The guards slowly walked away from the cage, pulling the rope tighter, chanting "Pull! Pull! Pull!"

With her last breath, she shouted, "All you demons will lose the war against God! I promise!"

Soon, her body hung three feet off the floor, her neck stretched out, her head dangling loosely to one side with her tongue protruding and her eyes bulging. Blood oozed from both eye sockets.

Four guards walked into the cage. The one who wore a chef's apron, wheeled a butcher's table in with Cutco carving knives. One guard held Dana and checked for her pulse, then announced she was dead.

The chef began carving her body for lunch. He used the same technique as with a turkey, knowing that some senators preferred legs over ribs.

The congress stood and cheered at the entertainment and lunch feast. The guards moved the cage behind the curtains again, where they would finish preparing Dana's body for lunch.

Satan called the meeting to order again, ordering all the cameras to be turned off.

"This is a very important time," he said. "After Passover ends, we face the final battle against God. It's inevitable that we'll lose more nonbelievers. How many is anybody's guess. We have key demons in positions in the houses of worship who'll be safe and ready to fight the final battle against God and His believers.

"Once the final battle is over, we'll kill all religious leaders in the world. Without political leaders, the religious leaders will turn to God for direction, and we must eliminate them, so that the last of the believers won't have anyone to follow.

"God will have a hard time communicating with His believers. That alone will cause more chaos. Bunker down at Vatican City and stay safe. We'll need all of you to win this war."

Chapter
SEVEN

Safe Haven

Immediately after Satan announced that demons and nonbelievers should take over the houses of worship throughout the world, they acted. By three o'clock that afternoon, they had control of all those places, though they were without electricity or ways to communicate.

Baby Jesus, Mary, and Joseph left their friend's home in Franklin Lakes, New Jersey, to be surrounded by a mob of reporters who began broadcasting live to their audiences.

Mary seemed to be only semiconscious, because she was listening to God and baby Jesus speak to her in a dream state and tell her what to say.

She spoke to the reporters in Hebrew, so none of them understood.

"Can anyone translate for us?" someone shouted.

A reporter forced his way through the crowd to stand beside Mary and Baby Jesus.

"What's your name?" someone asked him. "Who do you work for?"

"I'm Stan Klein. I'm the international reporter for the New York Times. I speak eight languages fluently. If you want me to translate what they say, I can translate it from Hebrew into English so all the believers in the world can understand."

"You're hired as the interpreter," Mary said in Hebrew, after hearing God tell her what to say.

Mary, holding the baby, became very emotional, dramatic, and animated, as she heard God explain His plan to achieve peace on Earth.

"I have achieved a miracle," Mary said, speaking for God. "I just brought Satan, his demons, and all nonbelievers voluntarily into houses of worship. Archangels will be sent to all those places at the beginning of Passover, the festival that marks the beginning of liberation of all good people from Satan.

"To those who are nonbelievers, if you don't become a believer in your God, you and your family will be sent to the sky and swallowed in a black hole created by Satan. You can't imagine the pain and suffering you and your family will endure for the next 666 years, the time it takes to go through the black bole. That's only the beginning for you and your families. Once you get there, you are interred in hell forever. The black hole will seem like a vacation compared to hell. You and your family will suffer excruciating pain forever. That is the choice nonbelievers face.

"During Passover, religious services in all houses of worship for nonbelievers will be ministered by Archangels Guinevere, Cassandra, Juliet, John Daniel, Lucinda Ball, Wayne, Cindy, Noel, Danny, Tom Howard, Alma, Lavana, Dave, Frank, Sharon, Pete, Frank and Sharon Ann, Greg, Ralph, and Don, Jay, Andre, Dolores and Darlene. Their mission is to convert nonbelievers to follow their God and baptize them into their religion. The archangels will be very successful in this mission.

"I know we won't be 100% successful in this mission. Our archangels will have trouble entering Vatican City, as well as five well-known houses of worship that hold a total of 80,000 nonbelievers, but we have a plan to deal with what's left of Satan's followers.

"Passover begins at six o'clock in the evening, Eastern Standard Time. Please place a symbol of God on the front door of your place of resident. That will show you're a believer, and the archangels will pass by your homes.

"If the archangels don't see a symbol of your God on the front door, you will be considered a nonbeliever and will be sucked into the black hole in the sky, where you and your family will be sent to hell for eternity. You have three hours to comply with these instructions."

She stopped speaking, and all around the world, believers quickly placed symbols of their God on their front doors. The TV reporters in the room with Mary stared in awe at the manifestation of God.

Nonbelievers panicked. Many tried to steal symbols of God from the front doors of their neighbors who were believers. Ron Stone found that out the hard way when he tried to remove a symbol of God from the house next door. A small lightning bolt struck him to the ground, leaving him dazed. When he woke up, he looked up and saw a black hole in the sky.

A moment later, he felt God grab him and lift him off the ground so hard, he shook like a rag doll. Ron slowly rose into the sky toward the black hole. He struggled to free himself, but God's power was too strong.

Ron looked around and saw the sky full of thousands of other nonbelievers who were floating toward the black hole. He screamed and cursed God, as he flew upward.

Demons watched the nonbelievers being sucked into the black hole, although they felt very nervous and terrified. The nonbelievers quickly saw they had only two choices—become a believer or flee to a house of worship with the rest of Satan's followers.

Demon Andy watched TV, which showed the nonbelievers being sucked into the sky and swallowed by the black hole to begin their eternal suffering. He didn't know what to do to save himself and his family.

Then he had an idea. He could pretend to be a believer in God. He could pray and go to church until everything calmed down, then he could go back to being a demon. Who would know?

He went to visit Steve, his neighbor, to ask if he could borrow his large crucifix to place on his front door. "Someone stole mine off the front door," Andy explained. "I don't want to confuse the archangels when they come around to check my house. They might think I'm a demon. That's the last thing I want."

Steve looked at him. "I didn't know you believed in God. I always thought you were evil. I remember you beating a child with a Fiberglas fishing rod for playing stickball in front of your house. When did you start believing in God?"

Andy smiled. "Yeah. I was having a bad day when that happened. I've always believed in God. I just have a different way of showing it."

"I never saw you or your family in church, not even on Christmas or Easter. I think you're trying to avoid being swallowed up in the black hole."

Andy grew angry. "OK. You asked for this!" He put Steve into a headlock and started punching him.

A small bolt of lightning struck Andy, knocking him down on Steve's floor. He lay there in pain, as a large, bright, white cloud appeared and vanished, leaving behind Archangels Sharon Ann and Frank, who stood around him in bright white robes that looked like they were on fire. The hoods were draped down the backs, revealing their heads.

They bent over Andy and looked at him.

"We've been sent by the Lord God to free the world of all demons and nonbelievers," Archangel Sharon Ann said softly. "You and all the other demons and nonbelievers can't fool Almighty God. Your plan to fake being a believer won't work. God knows when you're being sincere or when you're lying.

"Let this be a lesson to all nonbelievers. If you truly and sincerely believe in your God and follow Him, there will be a place for you and your family on Earth, the New Jerusalem.

"Andy, you, and your family are very evil people. Say good-bye to your world. You're about to leave it to spend eternity in hell."

"Can't we make a deal?" he begged. "I can repent. I promise. You can take my kids and my wife to hell, if you let me stay on Earth."

"Andy, you don't get it, do you?" Archangel Frank asked. "The mere fact that you're willing to sacrifice your wife and kids shows you're still a demon. Good-bye."

Something grabbed Andy's chest and lifted him off the floor, shaking him violently from side-to-side. The front door slammed open with a blast of hot wind, and Andy flew into the sky, heading for the black hole with scores of other demons and nonbelievers filling the sky around him. When he looked to one side, he saw his wife and children flying along with him.

Andy screamed for Satan's help, as he slowly rose into the sky.

Satan felt strangely nervous when he walked into Vatican City in Rome with 20,000 of his demon followers marching into the abandoned city.

It was the first time Satan and his followers ever entered that holy site. They looked around in amazement and felt curious enough to stop and touch the statues. Most of the demons had a premonition that God had somehow tricked them into coming there, where they would be placed into His hands.

Some of the demons genuflected and made the sign of the cross, then began praying to God before the statues.

A bolt of lightning struck the foot of the statue. When the smoke dissipated, Archangels Tom Howard and Fran stood there wearing bright, white robes that glowed so much they seemed like they were on fire.

"We've been sent by God to forgive all your sins," Archangel Tom Howard said to a praying demon, "if you are willing to renounce following Satan, believe in your God, follow His teachings, attend your house of worship regularly, and do good for your fellow man. God will then allow you to live in the New Jerusalem, where there will be peace on Earth."

Most of the demon army went down on one knee and became believers in God. Some thought they could fake it, but they were mistaken.

Archangel Fran turned to the ones who were lying. "God knows who a true believer is and who is not. Look up from the garden to the deep-blue sky. Do you see that black hole? All nonbelievers will soon leave this Earth and will be sucked into the sky to fall into that black hole, where you will enter hell for 666 years. Good-bye to all demons!"

Satan panicked. "Stop praying to your God!" he shouted.

Demon Captain Mark Zucker obeyed Satan's orders and began whipping the praying demons. When that didn't stop them, he took out his gun and began shooting them in the head, killing them instantly.

Satan received thousands of calls begging for help from his demons and nonbelievers who were being sucked into the black hole, but he ignored them.

Satan and his remaining followers marched through Vatican City and saw beautiful gardens ahead. The buildings all had statues of holy men and women on them.

Captain Mark killed so many praying demons, he ran out of bullets, so he beat those who were still praying with his empty guns.

The more he killed, the more demons joined their fallen fellows and began praying to their God. Almost all the demons were on their knees, praying for forgiveness. They promised to become believers and follow their God.

Satan looked around and realized God tricked him into bringing his demons into houses of Worship. God was about to win the war without firing a shot or using force. God's power could not be denied. Even Satan felt it and had to force himself not to believe in God.

Realizing he lost control of his demon army, Satan shouted, "Retreat to the sixth chapel in the city!" He had to resort to the last thing he could—natural disasters, floods, hurricanes, tornadoes, volcanic eruptions, earthquakes, tsunamis, and wildfires.

With a handful of his followers, Satan fled to the sixth chapel and locked the door behind them.

Chapter

EIGHT

Emergency Meeting

Satan and the thirteen demon followers who reached the chapel with him sat at a long table in the great hall. Right behind where Satan sat was the painting of the *Last Supper*. Satan and his followers were remarkably like the painting.

Satan came to his feet and faced the others. "I have no choice," he said angrily. "We must use all our evil abilities to bring the believers to their knees. I have total control of all natural disasters, including floods, hurricanes, tornadoes, volcanoes, earthquakes, tsunamis, and wildfires. I can bring misery to the entire world, but natural disasters are the only way we can win against God and His believers."

A small bolt of lightning struck the floor just across the table from Satan, raising a cloud of white smoke. It dissipated to reveal Archangels Cindy and Mel in white robes so bright they appeared to be on fire.

"Satan, God has sent us to ask you to repent and believe in your God," Archangel Cindy said. "We know you have violated all laws known to mankind. The misery and suffering you have caused to untold millions is beyond belief.

"You are the lowest form of life on Earth. If it was up to us, we would never spare you, but God is good and believes in forgiveness. We would love to see you burn in hell.

"God offers you this final chance to repent your sins. It will last for the next forty minutes. If you don't agree to become a believer by then, it's over. The same applies to the thirteen demons sitting at this table with you. To me, this offer is a no-brainer. Your choices are paradise on Earth or living hell for eternity.

"Your days are numbered. As we speak, all houses of worship that were invaded by your demons are being visited by archangels who are offering them the same deal. God tricked you into bringing your followers here. Think about it. How else could God get all your demon followers into places where they could worship their God? You aren't as smart as you think!"

"My demon followers will never become believers in their God!" he snapped.

"I know for a fact that Archangels Guinevere, Cassandra, Juliet, and John Daniels have reached a deal with over three billion demons to become believers in God. Only six demons in Notre Dame Cathedral have refused the offer. They're now on their way to the black hole, where they will spend 666 years of misery before arriving in hell for eternity."

"The clock has started," Archangel Mel said. "God will give you time to discuss your decision. We'll be back in forty minutes. Please vote for peace and harmony in the New Jerusalem. It's a win-win situation, where all the good people in the world will find peace on Earth.

"I believe we can achieve the same results with your demons. Please, Satan, renounce your evil ways and join your God for the good of the world."

"Satan," Archangel Cindy said, "we'll be praying in St. Peter's Basilica for peace on Earth. If you need us, call us on our cell phones."

She wrote down their numbers on some paper Satan had with him at the table.

"You have a lot of nerve to write on my official notes!" Satan snarled. "I can tell you our decision right now. It's no! We will never, ever become believers in God!"

"I move that we discuss the deal God just gave us," Demon Richard said. "Please, Satan, I beg you to let us vote on the deal."

Twelve of the demons stood. "Let's vote on God's deal!" they said.

Demon Judas stood to face Satan and the Archangels. "I would tell the archangels and God to go screw themselves. We still have all the natural disasters we can use. We'll bring the believers to their knees until they beg us to stop. Then we can turn them into demons."

Satan felt he had enough votes to deny God's proposed plan, so he ordered a thirty-minute hearing to discuss it with the demons.

"Your plan for natural disasters won't work," Archangel Mel said. "God will checkmate you on that, too. We promise.

"We're leaving now. We pray you change your minds and join us. We'll be back in forty minutes for your answer. We look forward to having all of you join us as believers in God."

Once the archangels left, the demons began arguing over what to do.

Demon Don stood. "Stan, why not accept the offer? I don't know about the other demons, but my family and I are sick and tired of evil and all the misery we have inflicted on the believers in this world."

Demon Judas fumed but waited for his turn to speak.

Satan rapped the gavel against the table. "Order! Order!" He stood and faced the thirteen demons, muttering to himself. Finally, he said, "Demons, we have to get ourselves organized or we'll lose everything we've worked so hard for. Does anyone have a suggestion?"

Demon Richard stood. "We have no choice but to surrender to our God and become His followers."

Satan cut him off before he could say more. "Approach the bench."

Demon Richard walked up to Satan, who was furious.

"Stand at attention and look straight ahead," Satan said.

Satan walked behind Demon Richard and took out a long, gold knife, grabbing his hair to pull his head back. With one stroke, he cut off the demon's head.

Holding the head in one hand, dripping blood, he turned to look at the others. "Anyone else want to surrender to God?"

Demon Gary Robbins, who was in pain from his recent mesh stomach surgery, was assisted to his feet by the demons beside him. "Don't you get it? We lost the war. I don't know about the others, but I plan to follow my God and become the best Christian I can." He shoved the others aside and moved as quickly as he could toward the door. He was like OJ Simpson playing for the Buffalo Bills, stiff-arming and running around the ones who tried to stop him. He made it out the door and raced toward the Sistine Chapel to be baptized.

After the others calmed down, Satan said, "Look. We have no choice. I have to use our last weapon against the believers—WMD."

Demon Judas stood. "What's that?"

"Weather of Mass Destruction. I can create natural disasters around the world. The followers will be devastated. If they don't surrender, they'll have nothing to return to. The war with God will be over within twenty-four hours. If the natural disasters don't work, I have a doomsday plan to destroy the universe. One way or the other, they won't have anything to come back to.

"I have to leave to warn my wife and kids to prepare for the aftermath from all the natural disasters. At least one-third of the Earth will be destroyed. My final doomsday plan will take a week to set up, so we must hold off God and His believers that long. I hope we make it.

"When those archangels return, they'll know that over ninety percent of the Earth will be destroyed. With that knowledge, we can negotiate a better deal with God and the survivors."

Demon Nikita stood. "I've known you for over a century. I didn't know you're married and have kids."

Satan stopped. For the first time, he showed a softer attitude. "Nikita, my friend, there's a lot people don't know about me. Since we're looking at the end of the world as we know it, I want you to know that I have enjoyed many evil women on Earth, but I fell in love with one particular woman. If I mention her name, you would recognize her for the evil she has done. I love her and my four kids very much. That's why I want to make sure she and the kids are safe. It won't take more than five minutes."

He left the room to call his wife and kids and to start the natural disasters. He also prepared to start his doomsday plan.

The rest of the demons debated what to do. They shouted at each other, and some started fist fights. Demon Judas sat at the table without a word, watching the chaos around him.

When the others finally paused, Demon Judas nonchalantly took the gavel and rapped the table once. "Stop this nonsense! You won't accomplish anything by fighting and screaming at each other.

"Let's sit down, take a deep breath, and get to work. We have very little time before Satan and the two archangels return. Does anyone have a suggestion how we can accomplish our goal and regain control of our evil empire?"

Demon Juan stood. "I have a good idea. Let's get the hell out of here and become believers."

All the demons stood, ready to run.

"I can't believe we had billions of followers, and now Satan is down to a handful," Demon Judas. "It's just him, me, and his wife and kids."

The door burst open, and Satan ran in. "I can't believe this! My wife and kids just left me for their God!"

Demon Ali put his hands over his ears. "This is all Satan's fault. We have to surrender as soon as possible to our God. Even if we win the war against the believers, Satan's doomsday plan means we won't have anything left to come back to. The universe as we know it will be gone. Guess what? That includes us, too!"

"Please!" Satan begged. "We can win the war against God. I just started all the natural disasters. They will wipe out most of the believers and their lands. Just give me one more day. The believers will beg us to help them."

Demon Raphael stood and stared at Satan, who had lost his power until he looked weak and humble. "Satan, I've made my decision. You can shove your demon life up your ass. I quit. I will be a true believer in God. You can do what you like to me, but I'm a believer now. I will leave and join the others in my faith. Good-bye. You're bluffing about that doomsday plan."

He walked out without any interference. The demons were shocked when Satan didn't do anything to stop him.

Satan sank into his chair and curled into a ball, crying bitterly.

The other demons walked out and headed toward the Sistine Chapel except for Demon Judas, who approached Satan and placed his left hand on his shoulder. "We must win this war against God and His believers. Let's get to work."

Satan looked up with his eyes streaming. "We've lost everything. There's no hope."

That was the first time Satan showed any sign that he didn't think they could win the war. Demon Judas lifted Satan off his chair and slapped him several times.

"OK, Judas," Satan said, calming down. "Thank you for helping me get organized. The two of us can still win this war against God and His believers."

Demon Judas looked at him, then laughed. "You really have a doomsday plan?"

Satan nodded. "Yes. The entire universe, including Earth, will be destroyed in a week if we can avoid being arrested. I need one week to make it happen."

"We're an army of two. You can't be killed, because you're a fallen archangel, but I'll be dead within hours, maybe a day. I know what I'm getting myself into. Let's fight for our cause. The only life I know is evil."

Satan nodded and drew himself back together. "Lock the doors. I'll start the WMD and get the doomsday plan ready. We'll put those believers in fear of their lives."

They looked at a TV set at the far end of the table, tuned to CNN. The reporter stood outside the Vatican, telling the world what was happening.

"Archangels Mel and Cindy have told God that Satan launched a weather and cyber-attack against Earth," he said.

Satan turned to Judas. "We just got free advertising for the entire world. Just hearing about the WMD attack will create panic everywhere."

Another TV camera showed the Sistine Chapel, where Satan's demons were being baptized at the altar. There were so many, Archangels Mel and Cindy needed extra help. God sent several dozen to assist them in baptizing the tens of thousands of new believers. Once someone was baptized, he helped the archangel baptize the next person, making the process go faster. That freed up some of the archangels to visit new believers at their places of worship around the world, not just at the Vatican. Within an hour, ten million new believers were baptized.

Satan looked at his watch. "The attack begins in ten minutes. I don't know why CNN talked about the cyber-attack, but I like that idea. I'll start that right after the natural disasters begin. I must be getting old. I should've thought of that."

They sat at the table and snorted some cocaine, watching TV occasionally and waiting for the natural disasters to begin.

After five minutes, nothing in the world changed. Satan kept checking his watch. When ten minutes passed, he and Demon Judas began to panic.

Satan screamed and cursed the TV set. He took off one of his sandals and banged it against the table in rage, then he ran up and down the room, screaming and cursing.

"What happened to all my natural disasters?" he shouted.

On the TV, the reporter was interrupted by a news flash that went inside the Sistine Chapel, where Archangels Mel and Cindy were being interviewed by Wolf Blitzer.

"God has stopped all the natural disasters Satan and Demon Judas tried to perpetrate on the good believers of Earth," Archangel Cindy said.

Wolf was amazed, but he remained professional, turning to Archangel Mel, who said, "This is for Satan and Demon Judas, who we know are watching this broadcast.

"As of now, Satan, you've lost all your evil powers. God took them from you. Your time is up. Come out and surrender, or we'll come in and arrest both of you. That's a direct order from God."

Satan and Demon Judas began accusing each other of gross negligence.

"It's over!" Demon Judas snapped, staring directly into Satan's eyes, something no one ever dared do before. "God and the good people have defeated all the evil on Earth. I plan to surrender to God. I will give them a good story about how I've become a believer and will follow Him.

"Once I prove I'm a believer, I'll come in to arrest you. I'll bring you before those two archangels, who will be happy to place you in custody. Once I hand you over, they won't have any way to know I was lying. As soon as the situation calms down, I'll start an uprising against God. You're on your own. I quit."

"Judas, your plan has one big problem." He grabbed Judas with one hand and pulled out his sword, hacking at his arms and legs. Judas collapsed, bleeding profusely.

"I hope you burn in hell," he whispered, as he died.

Satan jogged to the telephone desk and called the cell number the archangels gave him.

"Hello, Satan," Archangel Cindy said. "Can I help you?"

"Archangel, I want to surrender. What should I do so I won't be harmed?"

She looked at the cell phone, then handed it to Archangel Mel, who worked in law enforcement his entire life. He put the cell phone to his ear.

"Satan, I don't want any tricks from you. Got it? You have to strip down to your underwear. No shoes, socks, or hat. You lay on your stomach spread-eagled on the floor facing away from the door and show me your open hands. You'll obey all my orders. I'll come in alone, and you'll surrender to me. If you try anything, your negotiation with God will suffer."

"I promise to obey, Archangel Mel. I'll surrender to you and your God." In a tear-filled, sad voice, he said, "Please don't hurt me when I surrender. I have to go to the bathroom. Can you give me an extra ten minutes?"

"You made the right decision. I'll give you fifteen minutes."

"I promise to obey your orders." Then his voice became stronger. "I promise to work for peace on Earth."

He had fifteen minutes to change the situation and win the war against God. He quickly changed the password on his computer, along with various settings, then he opened the computer program called WMD. He didn't have time to pick the countries or the oceans where the natural disasters would occur.

He hit *Enter,* and there was an explosion. The Vatican filled with smoke from a nearby volcano that erupted, sending lava and ash toward the Vatican and the surrounding area. It reminded him of Pompeii in 79 AD, in the Campania region of Italy, a few hundred kilometers away. The lava and ash from that volcano buried the inhabitants alive and killed everyone in the city.

The TV at the end of the table suddenly showed people screaming and yelling. CNN reported the start of natural disasters around the world, killing millions of believers. Everyone knew who did it.

As Satan turned toward the door, Archangels Mel and Cindy ran in, followed by new believers. They grabbed Satan, and a woman in her nineties went down on all fours behind Satan's legs. The believers holding onto Satan shoved him over the elderly woman's back, and he fell hard, striking the back of his head. He lay there, semiconscious, moaning in pain.

"What have you done?" Archangel Mel asked. "You gave your word you'd surrender and make peace with God. I haven't cursed since I became an archangel, and I hope God forgives me, but you're a piece of shit and deserve everything that's going to happen to you."

Satan held his head, trying to stop the bleeding. "All you believers will die."

"Satan, stop the disasters, or God will!" Archangel Cindy said.

"No. I won't do it. Even if God wins this war, there'll be nothing left to salvage."

"Do you want to bet God will stop the disasters and win the war?"

"I'll take that bet."

White smoke around the Vatican appeared, then slowly dissipated, and soon, everyone could see again. The building shook, but they all knew that the smoke and vibrations were caused by God, not the volcano.

God appeared, with twelve of His disciples who represented all the organized religions of the world. Included in the group were baby Jesus, Mary, Moses, Buddha, Muhammad, and many others.

All believers faced their God and disciples, genuflecting with their right hands over their hearts.

"We're all believers!" they shouted. "Thank You, God, our savior!"

Satan, who was pressed against the floor by four big, strong believers, his head wound still bleeding, looked up and asked, "Are you here to surrender to me?"

"All believers stand and take a seat," God ordered. Glancing at Satan, He became visibly angry.

God spoke in all language simultaneously, without need of an interpreter. Everyone in the room heard him in his native language.

God faced the TV cameras and cell phones that were streaming the event. No one had ever seen Him before, just paintings of His image.

They were surprised that he looked exactly like each person who looked at him, as if they were looking in a mirror. Some remembered the Bible said they were made in God's image.

In a strong voice, He said, "Please, all believers take a seat at this table, so we can have a trial. I want you and the world to witness this. Everyone in the room will be sworn in as the jury."

He turned to Satan. "Satan, I made a monumental mistake hoping I could change your evil ways when I ordained you as an archangel. All believers know that God can do only good, helping people in need and never harming My believers. I can stop all natural disasters in the universe.

"Satan, I'll get back to you for the evil deeds you performed against good believers. Right now, I have more important things to do."

He closed his eyes and started praying. Within seconds, reports came in that all the natural disasters had stopped.

Wolf Blitzer turned to weatherman Chad Myers, who pointed to a world map showing that all the disasters had suddenly stopped. Perfect weather appeared in all parts of the world, making a first in history.

Wolf Blitzer was puzzled. "How strange that we don't have any bad news to report," he told Chad. "There are no wars, crimes, or anything negative. All the news feeds have nothing but good news. All diseases, including cancer and diabetes, have been cured.

"That's just the beginning of the good new pouring in to CNN. Please stand by. We have a news bulletin that poverty has also been eliminated. Wow! All the debt in the world has been wiped clean."

People stared at their TV sets around the world. Loud cheers went up in all countries. Believers began gathering in famous locations worldwide.

Every ten seconds, another CNN bulletin appeared, announcing the end of disabilities and terminal diseases. All people were cured.

Staff and visitors inside the CNN studios began cheering, and the studio audience couldn't help celebrating all the good news.

Wolf Blitzer was handed an endless stream of slips of paper from his staff, so he could give more announcements of good news to the audience.

"Since there is no need for government, courts, or prison anymore, all government buildings worldwide will become houses of worship and meeting places or study halls for believers to congregate and discuss God's teachings. All government parks will be turned into paradise places of worship.

"God has rid the world of all evildoers. They're on their way through the black hole to hell. Only one is left—Satan—but he will be taken care of after the trial.

"All armies and law enforcement groups have been disbanded. As of this moment, all firearms have been made unusable. God has cured drug addiction around the world. Since we don't need drugs anymore, they have been banned. There will be no illnesses or injuries. Lawyers and judges are no longer needed, either Since there are no taxes to collect, all taxes and tolls have been abolished.

"God has ordered there is no need for an army or law enforcement in the New Jerusalem because we will always have peace. Earth will become a paradise where all true believers will enjoy beauty, delight, and supreme happiness for the rest of their lives.

"God has promised to treat all believers as His children and will do whatever it takes to fulfill their dreams. All He asks is that they believe in Him and follow His teachings."

Satan, placed inside a cage, saw it all. Furious, he tried to use his evil power to stop God from curing illnesses, but it didn't work. His power was gone, taken by God.

Satan grabbed the bars and tried to shake the cage, but he quickly became tired and sat on the floor, crying, as God and His disciples continued praying at the table. The more they prayed, the more the Earth would become a paradise. There was nothing Satan could do to stop God's goal of achieving peace, tolerance, prosperity, and good health for all.

"I'm screwed," Satan said sadly.

Wolf Blitzer looked around the CNN studio, as it filled with white smoke. When it vanished a minute later, he saw everyone had their ages reversed to their twenties. His director, a man in his seventies, was suddenly twenty-three, and his clothes no longer fit. He had to hold onto his pants to keep them from falling down.

Phones in the studio began ringing, as women saw a much-younger Wolf and called to ask him for a date.

Wolf quickly reported what people had to do. "First, you must be a believer. Then you must pray to God and ask Him to reverse aging, putting you back to the age you want to have. It's painless, and in seconds you will walk out of a white cloud of smoke to find yourself much younger.

"This is a brilliant idea from God. Being young, we're all more productive. It's a win-win situation for us and the world."

Someone handed him another piece of paper with a bulletin.

"Please stand by," Wolf said, reading quickly. "God has announced there will be robots in every aspect of the world to perform manual labor. All believers will be drafted to work for two years supervising the robots."

He raised his eyebrows at the next line, then applauded. "There will be no discrimination in our new world. If a believer loves another believer, God will accept that. All religions will allow their clergy men and women to be married and lead normal family lives. God encourages families to have as many children as they want to populate the New Jerusalem. If any married couple can't have children, they can adopt up to eight children every twenty-one years."

He read another line. "Wow! Billions of planets in the universe will be the same as New Jerusalem, with the same climate, atmosphere, and amenities. We'll be able to travel and inhabit other planets. God has ordered that after New Jerusalem becomes overpopulated, some believers will be transported to other planets to make new lives for themselves and their families.

"A lottery will be used to determine the time and number of years believers must work. The names will be announced, and believers will work two twelve-hour shifts during a four-day work week. God has ordered that all construction projects be completed in less than four years to make this world a paradise. Our new world will be the stage, and the whole universe will be the theater."

The TV audience applauded and began chanting, "Paradise on Earth!" Soon, the words were picked up by viewers around the world.

"After the believer's two-year service, he will retire with full pay and health insurance for eternity. All believers will be inducted by the draft without exception. If you have any questions about the two-year work assignments or your retirement, call your local Social Security office."

The TV cameras kept reporting good news that lasted another six hours.

Chapter
NINE

God and His disciples stopped praying and turned to Satan in his cage. Cameras scanned the table and found Jesus had grown up into a mature young man with beard and long hair that resembled the picture of Him in the Sistine Chapel. Jesus was thirty-one years old.

God and His disciples performed endless miracles for six hours, then stopped praying.

"We must take a break," God said, "but there is still more to do for New Jerusalem. I order the Earth to be called by its new name of New Jerusalem. Let it be said and written in the new Bible that we have begun paradise on Earth. I want all believers in New Jerusalem to recognize your new leaders.

"As long as you believe and follow Me, all believers will never want for anything, and your dreams will come true. I want all believers to know that I have all the power to create this paradise and to make your dreams manifest. I can move mountains, change the course of rivers, make oceans, and create a perfect environment for living. It will all take place within the next four years.

"Your new leaders will hold a New Jerusalem service at the St. Peter's Basilica to achieve this paradise. The plans will fulfill My edict to create paradise on Earth. When I gave the world free will, history showed that you failed. All the wars, greed and evil in the world will cease to exist as of this moment.

"To all the believers in our New Jerusalem, we are all the same. We all drink the water and breathe the same air. There will be no more discrimination. Bless you!"

God looked at Satan in his cage, then He stood from his chair. "I can't defrock you as an archangel, but I can strip you of all your powers. As of now, you are excommunicated from all religions on Earth and in this universe. Your evil powers are gone.

"You know why we're here. Your time is almost up. You have been indicted on most of the horrendous crimes in the history of the universe. Since you're a fallen archangel, you can't be killed, so I'll make a special case of you."

God ordered the other archangels to surround the cage Satan once used to execute his demons and move it to the center of the room. The charred, rusty cage was wheeled forward, where everyone in the room would have an unobstructed view. The witnesses sat at the front table.

God sat at the head of the long table and ordered, "Satan, stand up."

Satan refused to move.

One of the four large believers standing around him said, "We can physically pick you up off the floor and force you to stand. It's your choice."

Satan looked at them and slowly stood. The four believers took their posts around the cage. Satan ran around the perimeter, screaming and cursing God and all His followers.

He held onto the bars, staring at the crowded room. "I object to this trial on the grounds that you have no authority over me on the Earth."

"There is no more Earth," God replied. "It's called New Jerusalem. Satan, your motion for a mistrial is denied."

Looking at the crowded room, He ordered all those in the room to stand and raise their right hands, so they could take an oath to be fair and impartial in fulfilling their duties as jurors.

God held up a criminal complaint that was almost sixty feet tall. It almost touched the ceiling of the Sistine Chapel. On it was a list of all the crimes Satan committed since he went to Earth.

God read them aloud for thirty minutes, then stopped and turned to the judges. "Will you accept this list as being true and accurate, so I don't have to read the whole thing?"

All twelve disciples accepted the complaint as it stood.

"I object!" Satan shouted. "The full complaint must be read, so I can defend myself."

"You'll have plenty of time to read it in your cage. Motion denied," God said. "Let me summarize what Satan has done. All the misery, suffering, war, and genocide that occurred on Earth was directed by Satan and fulfilled by his evildoers. We could go into detail with eyewitnesses or video recordings of the most-horrifying events that good people endured, but I'm sure the jury understands the gist of Satan's actions in the world. Do the members of the jury want me to give more detail?"

"No, God," the foreman of the jury replied. "We agree it's a waste of time to read the full complaint. We the jury agree there's more than enough evidence to prove beyond any reasonable doubt that Satan is guilty of all criminal charges."

God looked at the jurors and spread His hands. "Should we have Satan defend the charges, or should we just proclaim him guilty and avoid wasting time?"

"That's not fair!" Satan said. "I have the right to provide a defense and to read the complaint."

"Satan, giving you a trial is a waste of time, but you're right that in the New Jerusalem, there are rules. We've got a lot to do over the next four years, and we don't have time to give you a trial right now. Your trial is postponed for four years. We can't stop our plans to build paradise in the New Jerusalem. The time interval will give you the chance to read the millions of criminal complaints against you.

"I order you and your list of complaints to tour the world, where all believers can tell you what they think of you and your evil ways. You can witness the paradise in the New Jerusalem. You have no power to stop our achievements."

God nodded; the believers loaded the cage that held Satan onto a truck waiting outside.

"I'll see you at my trial in four years!" Satan shouted.

"I look forward to it," God replied. "Enjoy your tour. I hope and pray this teaches you a lesson. Good always prevails over evil."

Satan and his legal papers left the Sistine Chapel for their long journey.

Paradise or Hell?

God looked at his twelve disciples and said, "I've been working on a master plan with architect Archangel Ralph to make our dreams of a new paradise come true. Please bring the plans to the table."

Archangel Ralph stood and presented the details of God's plan for paradise in the New Jerusalem. He handed out twelve copies of the plan and said, "Please study these. All of us are familiar with heaven, having spent many years there enjoying the most-beautiful place in the universe, as well as the peace and tranquility to pray to God. Our plans show that the paradise on Earth will be a replica of the one in Heaven. We moved mountains, changed the course of rivers, and made waterfalls just like the ones in heaven."

"I've been working on this plan for the past hundred years," God told them. "I'm fully satisfied with the hard work Archangel Ralph and his staff have gone through to achieve it. I have accepted his plans, and work will begin immediately.

"I also made major changes to the inhabitants of the world to achieve this plan. We started with Adam and Eve and evolved their descendants for billions of years to create today's believers. We started with the cave man, who had a distinct purpose, as did all his ancestors.

"Unfortunately, there was an emergency elsewhere in the universe, which prevented Me from watching over you for the last few million years. I'm sorry for not being more involved in the growth of Earth. You can see what happened, with all the bigotry, prejudice, poverty, and evil that came. That will change as of right now.

"I have issued a decree that all newborn children will be the 76,000,068th evolution of the world. They will be master builders who will turn the New Jerusalem into a paradise. All will have superhuman intelligence, with minimum IQs of 188. That was also Albert Einstein's IQ. Those new children will grow to be six-feet-six-inches tall.

"Before I forget, My plan includes a factory to build robots to do most of the work for constructing the New Jerusalem. This will make life as easy as possible for all believers. Most chores and other work will be done by robots. They will diagnose and perform all medical procedures, as well as drive cars, fly airplanes, and command ships to deliver all necessary goods to believers. There will be no need for believers to work.

"I will ask them to follow My teachings and attend their houses or worship at least once a week. They must help other believers and do good in the New Jerusalem."

God began communicating to the entire world. "I ask all people to go to their houses of worship right now. You'll be given instructions where to report and what time to start work on the New Jerusalem. Please stand, raise your arms, and bow your heads. Close your eyes and pray with Me. There will be no more kneeling to your God. That was a manmade order, not one of Mine."

He recited the Lord's Prayer. All followers prayed aloud. When they finished, God spoke into an iPhone that helped transmit His broadcast around the world.

"Please go to your houses of worship now," God said. "We have all your essential needs ready, including food, clothing, and other things for a good life. Your house of worship will become the center of your needs from now on."

Mike and Holly finished praying with God on the Internet. They heard His final announcement, and Mike asked, "Should we pack our bags and go to our synagogue?"

"It's not that far," she replied. "If we need anything, we can come back to get it. Let's go see our God."

They put on coats, hats, sunglasses, and locked the door to drive to their synagogue. They noticed that the sun shone more brightly, and the deep-blue sky had few clouds. The temperature and humidity were perfect.

As they turned the corner and approached the main thoroughfare, they felt a sense of happiness and total peace at the sight of the many waterfalls on each side of the roadway, surrounding them in gorgeous gardens that weren't there the previous day.

They drove past the waterfalls and gardens, surprised at seeing the hundreds of robots working diligently. They usually listened to music when they drove, but it was a special day. They turned on the radio and heard a news anchor reporting that God appointed Archangel Noel to oversee all robots in New Jerusalem.

"Our God has given Noel his instructions to find a way to merge robots into believers' everyday lives," Archangel Noel said. "His goal to make all believers in New Jerusalem feel joy in life and to make our world a stage with the entire universe as the audience."

Mike turned to Holly. "Wow! Holly, pinch me. I must be dreaming. Can you imagine living in a world without war, where there is tolerance, good health, and no disease? We'll have long, healthy lives filled with prosperity and happiness."

"You just defined paradise," she replied.

Passing a church, they saw the parking lot was full of cars. There wasn't a single space left. The believers were polite to each other, as they left the church carrying gold booklets. They greeted each other with handshakes, pats on the back, and smiles.

"Is that the mean neighbor who lives next door to us and never speaks to anyone?" Holly asked.

"Yes, that's Tom. I can't believe he's in such a good mood. God is doing a good job. I haven't seen Tom smile in the twenty-five years he lived next door. All he did was call the cops when kids played on the street in front of his house. I never remember his having a good word for anyone."

Tom saw them passing by and jumped in front of the car, forcing Mike to slam on the brakes to avoid hitting him. Tom laughed, both his hands on the hood, then he walked to the driver's door. Mike lowered the window.

"I almost hit you," Tom said. "I could've killed you."

Tom laughed and shook his head. "I spoke to my God in church. He told me I can't die no matter what I do.

"I just wanted to say that if there's anything you and Holly need, please call or come over to my house. I'll help any way I can. I promised God I'd do only good deeds from now on. You've got a cracked sidewalk in front of your house that the city was giving you trouble over. I'll fill in those cracks once I get home. I promise.

"We live on a corner. The sidewalks over 200 feet long. Some of the estimates for the repairs were as high as $15,000. That's a big job," Mike said. "I'll help if you want."

"That's not necessary. I feel I owe it to you after being such an awful neighbor all those years."

"What can I say? Thank you!"

Mike and Holly drove off.

Holly looked at the believers leaving the church with large gold books. "Those must be God's instructions and assignments to build paradise in New Jerusalem."

They arrived at their synagogue and saw the parking lot was filled with cars, pickups, and buses. Mike drove around the block to find a parking space. He saw brake lights come on up ahead and felt someone might be leaving, and he was right.

"Are you leaving that space?" Mike asked, seeing the driver, his wife, and four kids in the car.

"Yes. Are you here to attend services at the synagogue?"

"Yes, we are. What can we expect?"

"Hi. I'm Herbie. This is the first time I've attended services in the synagogue since I was thirteen for my bar mitzvah. I'm forty-seven now. My family only attended for weddings and funerals.

"I'm ashamed to admit we never went to the synagogue even on high holy days. That just changed. Now we're members in good standing and will attend regularly. I promised Moses and God that we'll work for the good of the community. You won't believe this, but I just spoke to Moses!

"He told me what he expects from me and my family to achieve paradise in the New Jerusalem. I went into a deep sleep and dreamed I saw Moses sitting beside God. I never felt so at peace and safe in my life. Moses came up and shook my hand. 'Herbie, welcome back to your God.' He handed me a golden Bible. When I woke from the dream, I had the Bible in my hand."

Herbie paused and lifted a gold Bible from the car seat beside him. "Good luck, you two." He drove out of the parking space.

"Thanks for all the information!" Mike called. "God bless you and your family!"

Chapter

TEN

The Synagogue

Mike and Holly parked, and then they walked back to join a long line of people waiting to enter the synagogue. As they waited, they saw many believers leaving the building with golden Bibles in their right hands and legal documents in their left, which many tried to read, as they walked to their cars.

"I'll bet that legal paper is their instructions and assignment to make our world into a paradise on Earth," Mike told Holly.

"It's not Earth anyone. It's now the New Jerusalem. I think you're right. Those must be their new assignments. The people in the New Jerusalem are the luckiest people in the universe.

"We'll live our lives in paradise, and God will take care of us. He has good will for all believers. The evil people are gone except for Satan, and he's locked up on a tour of the New Jerusalem to see all the peace and happiness in the world. Can you beat that?"

After waiting in line for twenty minutes, Mike and Holly were greeted by Rabbi Albert, who gave Mike a *yarmulke* to wear, while Holly was given a hat. All the seats were taken, and the rear was filled with worshippers who stood four deep behind the seats.

In front of them all was Moses, wearing the traditional clothing of 1392 BC. He held two Torahs, and the Hebrew Bible lay on a table before him. He had his wife, Zipporah, and his children, Eliezer and Gershom with him.

Rabbi Albert walked up to Moses and shook his hand, then he introduced Moses and his family to the crowd. The audience's cheer lasted several minutes.

"As of now," the rabbi said, "we have a new world in which to live. I want all you believers to enjoy your lives of fun and happiness. I've got a joke for the occasion.

"A mother woke up her son and said, 'You have to get up and get dressed to go to the synagogue.'

"He replied, 'No, I'm going back to sleep.'

"Fifteen minutes later, she came into the room and woke him up again. 'It's getting late. You have to dress and leave your room.'

"When he didn't come down for breakfast, she went back to his room and shook him. 'Hurry up, or you'll be late for services!'

"He said, 'I won't go. The congregation doesn't like me, and I don't like them.'

"'You don't have a choice. You have to go, like it or not. You're the rabbi!'"

Everyone burst out laughing.

The rabbi smiled. "I want to thank Steve for that joke. I hope and pray all believers know what we're getting into. We'll have total enjoyment in our new world, so starting right now, enjoy yourselves!"

The rabbi stepped away, and Moses came forward and looked at the TV cameras before speaking. "I want to thank our God for this opportunity to speak to all of you. We all know why you're here. Our God has given us a golden opportunity to live in peace, tolerance, and happiness in the New Jerusalem.

"In the new world, believers will want for nothing. All physical work will be done by robots, supervised by believers. There is no government. Law will be passed down by religious leaders appointed by God. All believers have their choice of the faith they wish to follow for the year. If you want to change faiths, that will happen on April fifteenth each year.

"There are no more tolls or taxes. All TV channels <u>are fee.</u> All believers will be issued a debit card that can be used to purchase whatever one needs or wants. This card has an unlimited balance. With those cards, poverty will be eliminated.

"All believers will have their choice of homes or apartments. There will be no bills to be paid. All rent, mortgages, and utility bills will be paid by God. There's no need for insurance, since there will be no natural disasters, wars, or crime.

"God has robotic decorators available to paint and furnish all homes with any décor the person wants. God has given us unlimited resources to accomplish the eradication of poverty.

"There will be no need of hospitals or doctors in the new world since there are no diseases or conditions that can cause harm or pain to anyone. Mental illness and cancer are things of the past. To all believers in the new world, go out and enjoy yourselves! The New Jerusalem is paradise.

"There is no need for automobiles. We have portals that can transport you from one place to another anywhere in the universe.

"Let me give an example. Portals are set up like airports. Believers check in after making a reservation to travel to another planet. Within ten seconds, the believer will arrive there. The good news is that you can bring any amount of luggage you wish. There is no weight limit.

"The believer shows up at the portal stop sign with a debit card. Once it is inserted into the machine, he types where he wants to go, pushes the travel button, and arrive at the destination within ten seconds.

"New Jerusalem will be the stage, with the entire universe as the theater. We will show you what can be achieved if you follow your God. We will issue your assignments and a new gold Bible called *The Book of the New Jerusalem*, which will supplement all Bibles and the Torah.

"One big difference is that the idea that religions can profit from the beginning of time was a misinterpretation of God's Word. There is only one God, although there are many different religions. All followers are correct in staying with their own religion. Where religious leaders made their mistake was in refusing to follow the idea that there is only one God. That's why God has issued *The Book of the New Jerusalem* to supplement other holy books."

He looked at the TV cameras. "The instruction I just gave to this Jewish congregation are the same that are being given to all believers in New Jerusalem by their own religious leaders. Please attend Bible study at your synagogues. It begins this Friday right before services."

He turned to his Archangels—Dave, Jr., Tona, Carlyn, and Cary. "Please hand out the new Bibles and assignment sheets to all families and individuals."

As the believers received their new documents, they thumbed through them while Moses continued speaking.

"I'll give you ten minutes with the new Bibles," Moses said. "I know you're all curious."

He sat down with his family and waited, speaking to them in a low voice to avoid disturbing the others.

Mike and Holy looked at their new Bibles. The first page was a dedication page, and they were surprised to find it was dedicated to them in God's own handwriting!

To My Dear Believers, Mike, and Holly,

I promise that if you follow your God, you'll live in paradise in our new world called the New Jerusalem forever in happiness, good health, and free of poverty.

God

Mike turned to Holly. "Wow. We'll have a beautiful life together."

She hugged and kissed him. "God bless you!"

After the personal dedication page, Mike turned to page one and saw at the top the Ten Commandments, followed by over 1,000 pages of what was expected of all followers to achieve paradise in the New Jerusalem.

They thumbed through it and saw what God wanted was what they planned to do, anyway. The important part was the follow the Ten Commandments and help their fellow believers whenever needed.

After the ten minutes were over, Moses called the services to order.

"I want to read the prepared speech God gave to me and all religious leaders of the New Jerusalem to be told to all believers.

"What God is asking you to do is the same as what most of you were doing your entire lives. Be a good person, worship and follow your God, and help your fellow believers. Every follower is the same but different. We all breathe the same air and drink the same water.

"We have total tolerance in the New Jerusalem. There is no discrimination over nationality, race, religion, sex, or sexual orientation. Every follower will be treated with respect and honor.

"Does anyone have a question? Please give your first name. We don't need your last name. God knows who you are. He can follow up personally with you."

Several hands went up. The four archangels moved through the crowd, each one carrying microphones.

"Thank you, Moses," one follower said, "for this opportunity to ask questions. I'm Julie. How and where should we worship God?"

Moses smiled. "That's a good starting question. Look at chapter two of *The Book of the New Jerusalem*. It gives places of worship and times for religious services. They're held once a week, with Bible study right before. You can attend your place of worship as often as you wish. It's entirely up to you."

"I have a follow-up question. What happens if a follower refuses to go to his or her place of worship?"

Moses' expression became serious. "That's a sign he or she isn't following his God. It means the person isn't a true believer. If that happens, the individual will be treated as a demon and sent to the black hole that takes him or her to hell.

"God doesn't force anyone to worship him, but that's the price followers must pay if they want to live in paradise in the New Jerusalem. All believers must follow their God. Have I answered your questions?"

"Yes, you have."

He looked around the congregation and chose Jill, who stood near the front. Archangel Carlyn handed her the microphone.

Jill stood up. "I want to thank you for taking the time to speak to us about what's expected in the New Jerusalem. I have a question I've been thinking about my entire life. Who is our God? Where does He come from?"

Moses was taken aback, then said, "That's a very good question. That's the first time I've ever been asked that.

"Before there was a universe, which means before time and before matter existed, we had a heaven inhabited by the archangels. One of them was named God. Another was called Satan. All the hundreds of thousands of archangels got along well.

"At one of the archangel meetings, which were held to pass laws to help other archangels, we came up with the idea we needed a leader. All laws had to be passed unanimously. Every archangel had veto power.

"It was an easy decision. Archangel God was unanimously chosen to be our leader. No other was as well suited. He was the perfect choice, because he always did everything, He could to help anyone. He was the smartest, most-compassionate, loving archangel in heaven.

"Archangel Satan was at that meeting, and he stood up to oppose the nomination. He nominated himself as our leader. He got only one vote, his own. The members laughed when they counted the votes and saw the result. The more the archangels laughed, however, the angrier Satan became. He wasn't thinking straight, because he could have stayed long enough to veto the vote to make Archangel God as our leader.

"Instead, he cursed all of us, swore that he would work from that day forward to stop God and His followers, and declared he would work for evil. He stormed out without voting on the next item. All of us immediately realized that without Satan, we could have a unanimous vote to elect Archangel God our leader. We made the vote quickly, before Satan figured out his mistake.

"Once the votes were cast, and Archangel God became our leader, He told us He wanted to just be called God from then on. He then made a proposal to create the universe, which passed unanimously. He told us we should populate the new planet, which He called Earth, starting with Adam and Eve.

"That plan was also passed unanimously, and that was how Earth was created. Now for your other question.

"All archangels and God have a good sense of humor except for Satan. We all play games or have a glass of wine occasionally. Believe it or not, we live the same lives most people on Earth do, and we do many of the same things. The difference I see is that archangels aren't selfish and go out of their way to help their fellow believers any way they can. The other difference is that God and the archangels believe in peace and tolerance.

"I hope I answered your question."

"Yes, you did!" Jill said.

Moses looked around for other hands indicating questions. He pointed at Pete, who stood and asked, "Do you get along with and work with all of God's other religious leaders?"

"Yes. All God's religious leaders are the <u>Son and daughters</u> of God. I want everyone here to turn and look at each other. Everyone in this universe is the son and daughter of God. That shouldn't come as any surprise to any of you.

"What happens when you see God in your dreams? Whose face do you see? The answer is you see your own face. We're all made in His image. We're the sons and daughters of God.

"To get back to your question, all religious leaders not only get along, but we also love each other. We treat each other as brothers and sisters because we are. We all believe in one God, although we have different religious forms. That will change now. If you read your new book, you'll see that the only changes are that all religions will worship one God and follow the Ten Commandments.

"Believers can choose which religion to follow and can change their affiliation once a year. As long as believers attend their houses of worship at least once a week, all is well.

"I spoke to Jesus Christ, His father, Joseph, and his mother, Mary, and they said they were coming to meet us here at the synagogue right about now."

He stepped down to allow Jesus and his family to arrive. The congregation stood and stared. In an instant, all three stood at the front of the room.

Jesus, thirty-three, looked exactly like the pictures in most churches in the world. Anyone looking at Him would fall in love with his warm smile and soft voice. He was tall and thin, with long, brown hair that went to his shoulders and a trim brown beard that matched his hair. He had beautiful brown eyes and long eyelashes. He wore a white robe that glowed as if on fire.

Mary, Joseph, and Jesus hugged Moses. Mary kissed his right cheek. They shook hands, demonstrating their obvious love for one another.

Moses turned the congregation to introduce Jesus. The crowd gave him a standing ovation.

Jesus faced the cameras once the applause died. "I want to thank God and Moses for giving our New Jerusalem an opportunity to become paradise. You'll find that all religious leaders have been working together for a long time in heaven to achieve peace and tolerance in the universe.

"We were tied up with a big problem that lasted over two thousand years. It took up all of God's and our time to prevent the destruction of the universe. Earth was left on its own right after I was crucified. We solved the problem and then learned there was a big problem back here when people invented nuclear weapons.

"God and everyone in heaven was surprised that the people of Earth, aided by Satan, invented bombs that were capable of destroying the planet. That was when God changed the plan for the universe to achieve peace. He had to act quickly, or Satan would have destroyed the Earth before moving on to attack the universe. The new plan was that all planets would become exact copies of heaven, creating places for believers to live in paradise.

"I would be happy to answer any questions people have."

Half the congregation raised their hands. Jesus looked at Moses and joked, "I hope they don't crucify me."

Jesus chose Bert first.

"What was the major problem in the universe that took so much time to solve?" Bert asked.

"God will tell everyone what the problem was. He has a plan to inform everyone in good time. I promise."

"Can you give us a hint?"

Jesus turned to Moses. "Can we tell them what happened?"

"Let's bring in God to speak to the New World," Moses said.

God appeared beside Jesus. He simultaneously appeared beside all religious leaders in every religious center.

He wore a dark blue business suit with white shirt and bright red tie, black shoes and socks, and a black belt.

Everyone looked at Him and saw themselves. If they glanced in the mirror on the wall nearby God, they saw nothing. His image was blurred. People nodded, accepting the fact that God was made in their own image.

"First of all, please address me as Our Father," God began. "That's what I am, the father and grandfather to every living thing on this planet and in the universe. That's how I treat my children. I'm always there when you need me. You will never walk alone, I swear it."

Studying the worshippers, He was amazed at the amount of love he felt coming from them. He knew believers could now live without food or water for days, but they couldn't live without hope.

"I'm here in the New Jerusalem to fulfill all your hopes and needs. Believe in me. Please stand and sing *The Lord's Prayer.*"

After everyone in all the houses or worship sang, God said, "Please remain standing. Bow your heads and raise your arms above your heads with your hands open and pray with me.

"I will answer all your prayers. They will be granted within the next seven years. That will show you that all good people in the world will be rewarded for the good deeds they did and will do in the future.

"I have already granted the first few such prayers. Death is defeated. All believers will have eternal life. The fixed dates when believers enter heaven and or begin to age are gone.

"I summoned all the religious leaders here to show their believers that there is total unity to achieve peace, tolerance, prosperity and paradise in the New Jerusalem. I promise paradise will be completed in seven days.

"I know many were told by the TV news it would take four years, but that was wrong. That always seems to happen. I tell one religious leader to pass on My words to another. When they do, and it keeps passing between leaders, the final version is different from what I originally said. That happened many times throughout history.

"I found out that priests were ordered to be celibate. God never said that. What I said to Catholic Pope Gregory VII was that all members of the church need time to be alone with their God to pray away from family and friends.

"By the time my instructions reached him, however, they didn't reflect what I said. My instructions were taken out of context, and he received the wrong message, so he ordered priests must be celibate."

God gave more examples, including women's rights. He repeatedly sent messages to religious leaders that women had to be treated equally, but those messages were changed by the time they were received.

"Do you remember in the Old Testament when a religious leader misinterpreted what I said about what constitutes a family?" He asked.

"I told the religious leader that a family is two loved ones as the head of the family, not sister wives! I don't know if he took advantage of the situation or just missed what I said, but that took advantage of women from that time forward.

"Let me remind you of this crazy rule of sister wives. The rule was in the Old Testament Genesis, 2:22-24, and in the Mosaic law in Deuteronomy 21:1-17. That made it possible for a man to have more than one wife.

"King Solomon was the King of Israel from 970-931 BC, and he had 700 wives. He misinterpreted or took advantage of original ruling that two believers made up the head of the family.

"The oldest girl in the family had to marry first. If a suitor wanted to marry the youngest girl, he had to marry the other girls, too. That meant he could have as many wives as there were girls in the family. That also made women into second-class citizens.

"That's why I am here to supervise the building of the New Jerusalem. I don't want any more misinterpretations of My words. I just completed a meeting with all religious leaders, and we have agreed on my plans to build paradise.

"Now I'd like to answer Bert about what was so important that it kept Me busy for two thousand years. Right after my Son, Jesus, was crucified and sent back to me, we learned Satan had invented the nuclear bomb and planted over ten thousand of them in strategic places in the universe in the hope of causing mass destruction. He created a doomsday plan to destroy everything. We were shocked and had to neutralize all those weapons.

"All archangels worked day and night to find and neutralize those nuclear weapons. Satan never knew we did that. The last place we had to check was here on Earth, which is why I returned to supervise the destruction of those weapons. After that, we arrested Satan and sent his demons to hell.

"The problem was that he hid them very carefully. It took us over 2,000 years to find all of them and neutralize them. We thought we had them all until he set off three of them at the United Nations in New York City.

"He also gave the secret of nuclear bombs to his Nazi friends near the end of World War Two. He hoped that would help them win that war.

You should thank Me for helping certain Nazi scientists flee to America and develop the nuclear bomb before the Nazis had it.

"When countries have access to such weapons, it means the beginning of the end of the universe. We disarmed all planets that had any nuclear bombs. We had to stop Satan's doomsday plan. We succeeded, but it was close.

"We took away Satan's powers and ridded the Earth of all his demons. Now we're back and ready to create the New Jerusalem.

"The universe is perfectly balanced. All planets circle in regular orbits at normal speeds. If a nuclear explosion occurs anywhere, it upsets the balance of those orbiting planets. Soon, our universe would cease to exist. Time, gravity, and temperature would change forever. Life as we know it wouldn't be possible. If the world slowed or shifted is axis by even a little bit, it would eliminate all life.

"If Earth was destroyed by nuclear bombs, that would affect the balance of the rest of the universe. Satan was in the process of starting his doomsday weapon, and we had to stop him. That's why we returned.

"I hope that answers your question."

God looked around and nodded at another person. Archangel Tona handed her microphone to Evan.

"I was just curious about where Satan is now," Evan said.

"That's a good question. He's currently in Eastern Europe visiting all the large cities on the Danube River. I decided he had to witness all the good we can create when we make the New Jerusalem. Maybe he'll learn from the experience and see that believers can be happy and enjoy their lives. Believers will be allowed to speak with Satan in his cage and ask why he worked so hard to cause misery everywhere.

"I have reports that Satan is starting to answer questions about his motives. He said he believed he was better than anyone else and should have been elected leader of the universe. I call that being selfish.

"His claim is laughable. We had a fair election, not a rigged one like those in New York City. If you don't believe me about voter fraud and rigged elections in that city, <u>read</u> Mel Ladner's <u>nonfiction book</u>, *Human Error: Election Fraud*. He proves there is voter fraud and rigged elections.

"On the other hand, I received all the votes cast in paradise, with totaled over a billion. Satan will be tried when we have time. Until then, he has the chance to read a very long list of complaints against him. All believers will have their chance to ask him questions. We're calling it Satan's Magical Mystery Tour.

"Are there any more questions?"

Guy raised his hand. Archangel Dave, Jr., handed Guy the microphone.

"Father, I'm a New York City policeman. I have a question about my future as a police officer. What will happen to members of the army, police officers, politicians, and government workers? Will they still have jobs?"

"I have good news for you and all first responders, soldiers, and anyone who works for the government," God replied. "There is no longer a need for police officers, soldiers, or government workers. There are no wars and no crime in the universe anymore. All such agencies have been disbanded. We also don't have individual countries based on boundary lines on maps. We're all one nation.

"I'd like to thank all those who worked in those positions for the great job they did. You were needed. The benefits you earned are yours forever. The good work you did protecting believers in the world will mean you're at the top of the list to become archangels."

Albert stood, and someone passed him a microphone. "Our Father, we were issued new debit cards with a picture of You on the front, although they have our own faces. Does that card replace money? I also have another question to ask."

"Sure."

"Thank You. How do we travel in New Jerusalem to get from one place to another? Do we still have cars and public transportation?"

"I'm glad you asked those questions. The first one is about the debit card. It replaces all currency in the universe. There's no need for money. All goods and services are simply charged to that card. A true believer doesn't practice greed or gluttony. That debit card will prevent that from happening.

"Although there are no rules for greed and gluttony, we know what it is. To all believers, let your eyes be your guide.

"Concerning your question about travel, all cars and public transportation will be phased out over the next seven days. They'll be replaced by portal-to-portal transportation.

"I'm sure you're wondering what a portal is. For local transportation, there will be portal stops every four blocks throughout the universe. A believer goes to the nearest portal stop, enter his debit card, and types in his destination. In less than thirty seconds, he will arrive at his destination anywhere in new Jerusalem.

"It's a little different when traveling between planets. The believer must check in at his local airport and follow the same procedures as for local travel. The only difference is that he must start at the airport. All airports will be transformed into portal-to-portal universal transports within the next seven days."

Vivian stood to ask, "What do You expect us believers to do here in the New Jerusalem?"

God smiled. "The only rule is to follow your Bible and the Ten Commandments, be good believers, attend your house of worship at least once a week, and worship your God."

He stopped to look at the audience, seeing smiles on all the faces. Suddenly, people stood and gave God and His disciples a round of applause.

He waited for the applause to stop. "All believers in the world and the universe should pass the peace and greet each other."

Strangers met and greeted each other throughout the New Jerusalem, saying, "May peace be with you. Is there anything I can do for you?"

Those strangers immediately became friends and helped each other.

God was proud to see strangers becoming friends around the world and the universe. He told people they could text or email him at the number or email address listed at their house of worship, or they could speak to any of the religious leaders or God just by dreaming to have a conversation any time the person wanted. God the Father would always be there for them.

Chapter
ELEVEN

What a Difference a Day Makes

Mike and Holly made many new friends at the worship service after they heard Moses and God speak. It took half an hour to leave the synagogue. All the believers wanted to talk about meeting God and their religious leaders. The people Mike and Holly met were convinced that Our Father was right that their calling was to become better believers and to help as many people as possible.

They wrote down many email addresses and new phone numbers. Both of them wondered how they'd find the time to contact everyone they met.

After saying farewell to their new friends, they arranged to meet at the synagogue the following day to help the needy.

As they left, they saw that God's plan to achieve paradise was already affecting more of the landscape. New beautiful waterfalls and weather prevailed.

The stopped at the top of the synagogue steps and stared at the changes that occurred, during their three-hour meeting. Both felt happiness, contentment, and peace. They believed New Jerusalem would be filled with luxury. All poverty and misery would be eliminated.

Mike turned to her. "I believe Our Father hit a home run when He returned."

"You're right. I have next Friday on my calendar for attending service."

"Put me in, too. I want to come with you."

God, out of a sense of humor, named Satan's world tour the Magical Mystery Tour. Satan was furious when he found out about that, as well as what God expected him to do—defend all the bad deeds and misery he created.

Satan had lots of time during the day to read and study the criminal complaint against him. It took up half the cage. Millions of pages detailed all the crimes Satan and his demons performed.

Satan knew if God could prove only one of those crimes, he and his demons would be found guilty and would be sent to hell. That was the last thing Satan wanted.

He had little hope. The only thing he could do was stall and play along, meeting as many believers as possible on his world tour. After the tour ended, Satan would offer endless motions to the court to ask for appeals. He just hoped God and the believers would give him a break. He didn't care about any demons still surviving in the New Jerusalem. If they went to hell, it wasn't his problem.

The first leg of the journey started in Eastern Europe. He went to a riverboat on the Black Sea to begin his travels down the Danube. All countries in Eastern Europe followed communism until 1989. Satan and his demon congress created that form of government to take away people's freedom and prevent believers from worshipping their God.

Under communism, if more than five people gathered in one place, they would be arrested. All places of worship were prevented from holding religious services. The government also banned rock and roll music.

What made Satan proud was how the governments spied on each other. The communists picked up any citizen and demanded he give the names of ten people who worked to stop communism and tried to disobey the rules.

All of those people were sent to work camps and were tortured. If the citizen gave only nine names, the tenth person would be himself to help round out the quota. Satan knew people would give the names of innocent people just to prevent themselves from being sent to a work camp.

He was very proud of inventing communism. He promoted all the demons who worked on that bill once it passed the demon congress.

He looked out of his cage to where the boat sailed on the Danube. The scenery on both banks was a direct copy of heaven, with beautiful churches placed on mountains. Scenic views of waterfalls were everywhere. The buildings all looked new.

"What a waste that during the years of communism, those buildings weren't used except for public events, not religious services," he muttered. "Maybe I was wrong about communism."

He stopped and wondered, *What did I just say? I've been fighting against this since the beginning of time, when I ran for leader of heaven. I've been doing evil ever since. Now I'm starting to believe in God and having doubts about what I did to all the believers. I have to stop thinking like that.*

He looked at the pile of criminal complaints that took up half the cage that was his home. He moved a sixteen-foot ladder and placed it against the pile that stood eighteen feet tall, almost touching the ceiling. The papers were in alphabetical order, with the number of intendments at the top of the pile. All God needed was just one complaint that found Satan guilty, and he would be sent to hell.

He had to read a couple of the complaints to see if he had any hope of winning a trial. Climbing the ladder, he looked for criminal complaints against him from World War Two. Those would be near the top of the pile.

He found them quickly. They were the second document in the stack. He couldn't understand how the prosecutors found all their facts and evidence. It was true he committed the atrocities during the war, but he was baffled how they discovered the evidence against him.

As he read the complaint, he realized Hitler had to be an informer for the prosecutor's office. Hitler must've made a deal not to be sent to hell if he informed on Satan's crimes and plans.

He became convinced Hitler was the rat. He found audio tapes and 8mm film that eventually showed Hitler must've provided them. They all demonstrated that Satan was guilty of the accusations.

Just that one complains was enough to send him to Hell. There was no sense reading any more pages. He was finished.

He set down the World War Two complaints and began talking to himself.

"There's no way I won't be found guilty. However, if they offer me the chance to plead guilty of a lesser charge, I can stay in paradise.

"I have to stall, to kill time here in paradise for as long as I can and enjoy life. At the meeting with the believers, I'll answer their questions and try to charm them into thinking I'm on their side. Maybe that'll work. If I can get just one person on the jury to give me a favorable ruling, I'll be allowed to stay."

He sat at the table on the cage floor to eat scrambled eggs, bacon, buttered toast, and black coffee without sugar. He took out a pen and piece of paper to write down his plan to win over one juror.

"I'll go after a woman. I'm the one who made women second-class citizens when I changed God's rule about what a family was supposed to be. All the demons in the world praised me for that one."

He sighed. When he was in his twenties, he was the best-looking man in the universe. Women fell for him constantly. That's how he made so many good women do evil things and was able to ruin their lives.

That was still working until God and the archangels returned to Earth. He smiled at the thought of women falling in love with total losers who had no future or way of earning a living, just because the man was handsome. The truth was, those handsome men were demons. It was laughable that so many good women thought they could change a man into becoming a good family man. That idea was a myth Satan invented to control and ruin good women's lives.

He wrote a to-do list. He had to get back in good physical condition and become handsome again. That meant taking care of his personal grooming and dressing so women would fall in love with him again. He had little to lose.

He banged on the cage bars with his metal cup until Archangels Judy Lynn and Stan walked over from the guard room.

"Can we help you?" Archangel Stan asked.

"Yes. God said I can have almost anything I want to make my stay as a prisoner more comfortable. First, I want a mirror and a grooming kit to make myself presentable when I meet people to answer their questions.

"I understand that all conferences will be televised. I'll need clothes for that. I want three-piece suits, different color ties, alligator black belts, new black shoes, underwear, and black socks. I'll need some expensive gold jewelry, like watches, rings, and gold necklaces. Those were taken from me when I was arrested. Would you please return that jewelry to me, so I can be presentable to the universe?"

They stared, shocked he used the word *please*.

"I also need to get into shape. I want a dietician to prepare low-calorie meals for me. I'd like to be healthy and lose about forty pounds. I need a beautician to style my hair and beard, as well as take care of my fingernails and toenails.

"Since I'll be in the top news stories for the foreseeable future, I want a gym and track, so I can work out and get in shape. I'll need endurance to handle the stress and agony that will soon come to me."

Archangel Judy Lynn looked at Stan. "You're right that our God is loving and caring. He told us to make your stay as pleasant as we can, but we can't grant your requests. You aren't a believer. In New Jerusalem, there are only believers in our God. The nonbelievers are on their way to hell."

"We believers know about redemption and forgiveness," Archangel Stan said, "but we aren't stupid, either. You're the worst person in the universe. If anyone deserves to burn in hell, you do."

Satan stared at them. "What would happen if I changed and became a good archangel again?"

"What did you say?" Archangel Judy Lynn asked. "I don't think I heard you right. Did you ask about becoming a believer and a good archangel again?

"We have to get in touch with our supervising archangel. We'll relay what you told us and will get back to you with our boss' decision."

Opening the cage door, they led Satan to a special secure bathroom, where he found the necessities to shower and groom himself. After Satan finished, the two archangels couldn't believe the difference. Satan also took advantage of God's rule that he could choose any age he wished.

He became twenty-seven years old and went to his desired weight of 176 pounds. He stood six-feet-three-inches tall and had beautiful deep-blue eyes with a handsome face. He resembled a young Paul Newman.

When he walked out of the bathroom with just a towel wrapped around his waist, he looked like a male model with chiseled abs, stomach, and arms. The archangels couldn't believe how handsome he was.

Archangel Judy Lynn couldn't take her eyes off him. Like most women, she felt immediately attracted to him.

"Let's put lover boy back into his cage," Archangel Stan said. "I want to talk to you about Satan." He studied Satan, wearing only his towel. "I know what you're up to. You want to get one over on us, don't you?"

Satan used his new, sexy voice. "I'm being perfectly honest with you. I've had a change of heart and have decided to become a follower of God. I met good people in the last few days, and they impressed on me how honest they were, with good intentions to help others. The good people I've met couldn't have been nicer. I haven't associated with good believers since I left heaven millions of years ago.

"I made a mistake by endorsing evil against all good believers for all these years. Maybe I should ask our God if I could stop all the evil in the universe and become a good archangel again."

Archangel Stan was surprised. "That's great about wanting to stop evil, but how do we know you're serious? We can't take your word about wanting to follow God. You have to show us with good deeds and helping people. We need actions, not words.

"We'll pass on your new feelings to God."

They escorted him back to his cage and locked the door before returning to the guard room.

Satan sat at his desk in the cage and thought over what happened. *I'm confused,* he thought. *Do I believe what I just said about God, or am I just acting to stay in paradise? I just don't know anymore. What am I doing? Am I good or evil?*

I'll try being good and see how it works out. I can always be evil again.

Chapter
TWELVE

God Calls a Meeting

Archangels Stan and Judy Lynn called Jesus and told Him what just happened and what Satan said. He listened carefully. Archangel Judy Lynn added more details.

Jesus was very interested in what Satan said. "If he's telling the truth and wants to become a good believer, then our problems are solved. We'll have peace and goodwill throughout the universe. I'll talk to God and our religious leaders and call a meeting. We'll tackle this issue."

Jesus spoke to God, and they agreed to have a meeting at 3:00 PM at God's headquarters, a church established in 1958 on 71st Street North in St. Petersburg, Florida.

All religious leaders were there on time. God stood to face them and said, "I want to welcome you to My church and new headquarters here in St. Petersburg. All are welcome at our services every Sunday. I look forward to greeting you here. Let us pray."

All bowed their heads and raised their hands to pray.

When they finished, God said, "Let's get down to business. You'll heard the agenda about the issue of Satan becoming a good believer. Do you think he's lying, or is he serious about believing in Me, his God? Does anyone have any ideas about handling this situation and bringing him back to being a true believer?"

Moses stood. "Can we trust Satan? The answer is no. Send him back to hell where he belongs, the sooner the better, and without a trial."

Buddha stood next. "Moses is right. We can't trust Satan, but this is also a golden opportunity to achieve the goal we've been working toward since the beginning of time—peace, tolerance, and prosperity in the universe. We must give him a chance to prove he's telling the truth. There's a lot to gain if <u>he</u> becomes a good believer."

Jesus stood after Buddha finished. "We're all for redemption and forgiveness. I must agree with Buddha. Let's give peace a chance and see if he's lying. We can always send him to hell if he is."

Mohammed was next. "I'm on Moses' side. We should send Satan back to hell. I wonder if my fellow religious leaders have read the criminal complaint against him. It's millions of pages long. It's impossible to read the whole thing. Each paragraph spells out atrocities he committed against our God.

"For argument's sake, let's do the math and say there are six atrocities on each page. That means Satan committed at least twelve million atrocities against God and the good believers in the universe. That's a lot to forgive.

"I must advise You, God, that even if he's telling us the truth, he should be punished for his crimes against You and the good believers."

The religious leader of the folk religions asked for permission to speak. "I've heard both sides of this argument over what to do about Satan. I agree with both. Satan is evil, and we can't trust him to keep his word, but this is also a once-in-a-lifetime opportunity for peace and happiness in the entire universe.

"I hope I'm right in thinking that we must give peace a chance. We have to give him the benefit of the doubt and accept what Satan is saying."

The debate continued for six hours without a break, ebbing and flowing between the two opinions. Finally, when Jesus was making another argument to give Satan a chance, God interrupted.

"My Son, <u>you</u> made the winning argument," God said. "We must let Satan show us that he has changed. I will grant him six months' probation to prove to all that he is sincere about following Me as his God and becoming a believer.

"Let's bring him to my headquarters here in St. Petersburg and cross-examine him in front of the entire universe. We'll invite all the TV reporters, newspaper reporters, and Internet reporters. We'll air it live throughout the universe and ask for feedback from all good believers who are watching Satan's testimony. They can vote via the Internet whether they think he's lying."

Archangel Paul stood. "My Father, this has never happened before. You're saying that God has decided not to make a decision and let others do it for you. Are you sure You want to give up making this decision?"

"No, I'm not giving up the power of deciding about Satan. I just want feedback from our believers. The final decision will still be Mine. Either I'll give him a chance to redeem himself, or I will gladly send him back to hell.

"This debate is ended. Bring Satan here and have the hearing transmitted to all. That's final."

"I'm sorry if I made you angry, God," Archangel Paul said. "I had to speak up. It sounded like you would look weak to your followers."

"To be totally honest with you, I don't know how to handle Satan. I'd love to welcome him with open arms into the fold of all good believers, but how can I forgive all the atrocities he committed?

"Let's bring him in and see what he has to say about becoming a true believer. We'll ask him some pointed questions and see if we can discover the truth. It'll take one day to set up all the necessary equipment."

Archangel Paul looked at his watch. "It's eight o'clock in the evening. We can be ready by nine o'clock tomorrow night to transmit the hearing to the entire universe."

"OK. That's what we'll do. It'll be tomorrow at nine o'clock. Thank you for your work, Archangel Paul. I'm sorry I became upset with you, but you're right. I have to make the final decision on him one way or the other."

Archangel Paul left the room to begin preparations.

"We have some other unfinished business to attend to," God said. "Please have Archangel Ralph, the architect, come in with an update on building paradise in the New Jerusalem."

Archangel Ralph was escorted in by two archangel ushers. He walked to the front of the church and greeted his God.

"I looked out the window before we started our meeting and saw the progress we've made so far," God said. "Are we on schedule to complete the project in seven days?"

"Thank you, Our Father, for the opportunity to update you on the project of creating the New Jerusalem. We're on schedule to finished exactly on time. I want to thank You for the help with the robots and other equipment.

"We might actually finish in six days, but that's a long shot. I can guarantee we'll be done in seven. I have a short film to show you the progress we've made as of six hours ago. May I show it to You and the religious leaders?"

"Yes, you may."

A large screen descended from the ceiling, and all the religious leaders watched as the lights went out and the movie started, with Archangel Ralph narrating.

"As you can see, the housing for all the good believers is being constructed. The believer chooses the kind of house he wants. This means all homes are custom made. They choose the color for the exterior and interior, as well as the kitchen décor and all furnishings. We make their dreams come true by giving them their perfect home.

"The other good news is there are no restrictions on the way they live. They can have pets. If a dog barks, there is a volume control that automatically silences the sound. Believers can fly flags and have as many children as they wish.

"There will be no noise complaints, because we invented music that only the one playing it can hear, along with any others who wish to share in it. Since there are no cars, all parking problems have been eliminated. Good believers will live in peace and harmony in their homes."

God and the religious leaders, studying the images, saw that the plans required the movement of entire continents to make them closer together to take advantage of the milder temperatures near the equator.

Archangel Ralph stopped the movie for a moment to explain how and why they moved the continents. "With a perfect climate, growing healthy food for the believers becomes easier. All food will come from natural ingredients. We will offer no food that comes from animals.

"Drinking water will come from natural springs that are so pure, no one will wish for soda or other substitutes. Still, it's a believer's choice what he or she drinks, if the person wants to have something other than water."

He saw that the religious leaders had satisfied expressions. He started the movie again to show images of springs bubbling with pure water, aided by waterfalls that the workers recently finished. The beautiful landscapes reminded all of heaven, which they left only a few days earlier.

Finally, he stopped the movie. "As you can see, we have made an exact duplicate of heaven here in New Jerusalem." He turned toward God. "Thank You, Our Father, for choosing me to bring this project to completion for the believers.

"I'd like to mention to the religious leaders that God and I had a long talk about what He could do to improve the wellbeing of the good believers. I asked why they had to die just to enjoy heaven. Why couldn't they enjoy it while still alive?

"He looked at me and said that was a great idea. Heaven was getting overpopulated, and we needed to build another one or turn the universe into heaven. He even asked, 'Why didn't I think of that?'

"He asked me to draw up plans for New Jerusalem on Earth, an experiment to see if paradise could actually work in the universe. I started working on it immediately, supervising a staff of over 10,000 architects who worked day and night for forty years to draw up the final plans.

"Let me show you how well it has worked out." Walking to the big picture window on one wall, he opened the curtains.

The religious leaders stared in amazement when they looked out and saw a tall mountain that resembled Mount Hood in Washington state, with snow at the top. All along the mountain were gorgeous views filled with colorful wildflowers, waterfalls, and a large, deep-blue lake fifty miles across.

"Our Father has held this meeting for only six hours," Archangel Ralph said. "When the meeting began, the terrain in Florida was flat, with nothing higher than thirty feet."

The others laughed.

"We call them hills where we came from," God said.

"You can see how much progress we made in the last six hours. We completed over 80% of paradise in New Jerusalem."

He gave God a regretful look. "Our Father, I'm very sorry, but I have to get back to work so we can finish the project on time. I'll bring you updates as soon as I can."

"Keep up the good work," God said. "You're excused."

"Thank you, my God." Archangel Ralph packed up his materials and left the room.

God approached the microphone. "Next on the agenda is the question of how the good believers are doing in their new environment. Do we have any statistics on how many believers attended their houses or worship this week?"

Isaiah, Moses' son, was responsible for keeping the statistics. He walked up to the church altar carrying a spreadsheet.

"I'll let Isaiah give us this report," God told the others.

Isaiah stepped in front of the microphone. "Thank You, Our Father, for the opportunity to report on what we learned about how the believers feel about their new lifestyle.

"The good news is that our survey found we have 99.9% satisfaction among the believers in New Jerusalem. The remaining one-tenth of people who were dissatisfied are all former demons. We have their names and believe some are not sure if they wish to be true believers.

"Even if only one-tenth of one-tenth of the former demons turn against God, we'll have a problem. We would be right back where we began with war and strife. Satan could easily return, and we'd lost our chance for peace in the New Jerusalem. Unfortunately, we have no clear test to prove if a former demon has become a true believer. We can only take their word for it. During the survey, we learned that a few of the former demons are simply waiting for Satan to return and lead them against our God."

The religious leaders began talking among themselves. The main question they had was whether they could trust the former demons or even Satan to keep their word.

God stood. "Isaiah, what you just said is that Satan and his evil ways aren't done yet. That means peace and happiness will be impossible to achieve in the universe, and we're wasting our time trying to deal with Satan."

"My Father, that's what the statistics show," Isaiah replied. "Once a demon, always a demon. The residual rate for demons is 100%. When they have the chance, they'll return to evil and will follow Satan.

"Let me show you the statistics of how many went to their houses of worship this week. The numbers are the same as the overall survey—99.9%

attended their houses of worship. The same one-tenth of a percent didn't go. All those people were former demons.

"The numbers don't lie. I'm giving you my best advice by saying <u>you</u> can't take the chance and allow former demons to live in our universe."

"That's an eye-opener," God said, looking at the religious leaders. "Should we cancel the meeting with Satan, or do we want to hear what he has to say? I'll let you decide. Personally, I'd like the chance to question Satan about his intentions for the near future. Maybe we can get some personal information about him that we can use to stop any plans he might have."

Jesus stood. "My Father, our whole life we have believed in redemption and forgiveness. Why can't we give Satan a chance to redeem himself? Maybe he really has had a change of heart and will be able to lead the former demons to make them work together and create peace in the universe."

"My Son, you're right. We'll show Satan the same respect we should show any other sinner who wants to redeem himself and ask for forgiveness."

The religious leaders agreed, stating they wanted Satan to appear on schedule and see if he really had become a true believer and was willing to work for peace in the universe.

"Thank you all for attending this conference," God said. "My decision is to allow Satan to appear before us as planned. I'm glad we <u>settle</u> that. I look forward to questioning him tomorrow. I want answers to questions that have bothered <u>me</u> for centuries.

"Is there any other business concerning New Jerusalem we wish to conduct? If not, I say this meeting is adjourned."

No one spoke up. God struck the gavel once, ending the meeting.

Chapter

THIRTEEN

Satan

Satan sat in his cage, preparing for the meeting with God and the religious leaders. He wrote down his opening statement, then he stood before the mirror the archangels provided and practiced his speech until he had it down pat.

Sitting at his desk again, he highlighted certain parts of his speech that he wanted to emphasize. He decided to show more emotion when he gave the speech.

Back in front of the mirror, he practiced again, using his face, arms, and hands to indicate strong emotion at certain points.

He rehearsed it over hundred times and was finally satisfied that he had a good chance to sway a majority of the believers in the universe. If he got enough of them on his side, he had a chance to become a good archangel and stay in New Jerusalem.

He needed a break from his preparations, so he began working out, hoping to look his best before all the women in the universe. He wanted to make them fall in love with him and add their opinion to the total so he would be allowed to remain.

Archangels Stan and Judy Lynn interrupted his workout to deliver a three-piece black customized business suit for his meeting with God. He accepted the suit and black shoes, thanking them.

"I never saw anyone look as good as you," Archangel Judy Lynn said, giving him a once-over.

Satan's horns were trimmed and waxed. His long, beautiful black hair was parted on the right. When he turned around, even his long lion's tail was groomed. She realized he could become a heartthrob, and women throughout the universe would fall for him.

She turned to Archangel Stan. "Would you take a picture of the two of us?"

"Sure. Where do you want it taken?"

"We can unlock the cage and stand near the holy statues or just stand close to each other in front of the cage. Satan, what would you like?"

He thought for a moment. "Let's take it in front of the cage. I'd like the believers of the world to see the way I've been treated."

"Do you have a problem standing in front of the holy statues for your picture?" Archangel Stan demanded.

Realizing his words might be taken out of context, Satan quickly created an excuse. "I'm sorry I didn't tell you, but I hurt my left leg, and I have a little trouble walking. If you insist, I'll be glad to take a picture in front of the holy statues."

They weren't sure if they just caught him lying. Both archangels wanted to report the incident as quickly as possible.

"I'm ready," Satan said. "Are you ready, Archangel Judy Lynn?"

She acted like nothing happened. He came out without a limp, and she asked, "Where should we stand?"

"Let's pose in front of the holy statues," Satan replied.

Archangel Stan took the picture of the two of them before the holy statues.

"That will become a classic," Satan said jovially. "I can see it on posters and commercials throughout the universe." He laughed.

Placing him back in the cage, they locked the door.

"Thanks for the picture," Archangel Judy Lynn said. "We'll see you tomorrow morning. Good night."

Once he was alone, he muttered, "I might be falling in love with that archangel. It seems clear she's ready to fall in love with me. I doubt she'll make an issue of my not wanting to stand in front of the holy statues. I just hope they don't report this."

In their office, the two archangels debated what to do.

"I know he lied to us about hurting his leg and having a limp," Archangel Judy Lynn said, "but maybe he felt uncomfortable standing in front of the statues. He hasn't attended a religious service in thousands of years. Maybe we should give him a break and not report this."

"I could understand if he simply didn't want to stand in front of the holy statues," Archangel Stan replied, "but lying about his leg and having a limp? We can't sweep that under the table. The entire universe depends on finding out the truth if he's become a believer. We must report this to Jesus, and I mean right now."

Archangel Judy Lynn realized she was letting her emotions control her. Slowly, her expression changed, as she realized Satan was manipulating her into giving him a break.

"I'm wrong," she said. "God must know we caught him in a lie. I don't think we can trust him after all."

"I'm with you 100%. We have to call Jesus."

They called and placed the cell phone on speaker to report the incident and what they suspected about Satan.

"I'll tell God about this," Jesus replied when they finished. "We'll be ready for the meeting with Satan tomorrow. Thank you for this important information."

Satan exercised often, trying to look his best in front of the universe and hoping he could persuade enough women to fall in love with him and sway the vote. He remembered his propaganda about how women could change evil men into becoming good family men and laughed. Women were stupid if they assumed that would work.

Throughout the night, he rehearsed his speech and practiced his answers to the questions he expected he would get.

In the morning, Archangels Stan and Judy Lynn brought Satan his breakfast of oatmeal topped with honey and cashews and black coffee.

She looked at Satan. "You look good this morning. Did you sleep well?"

He looked back at her. "You don't know much about me, do you? I haven't slept since I became the devil. That's why God doesn't understand me. God communicates with people through their dreams. If I don't sleep, he doesn't know what I'm thinking or doing."

"It's like if you don't use the Internet and share personal information. Then people won't know who you are or what you think. You don't exist in their world and become anonymous."

"Why would you care if our God knows what you think or your plans about becoming a believer?" Archangel Stan asked. "Don't you plan to become a true believer?"

Satan looked puzzled. "That's my problem. I'm really confused about becoming a believer. I'm between a rock and a hard place. I need time before this meeting with God to make up my mind whether to become a believer or to rule all the demons in hell.

"I'm asking both of you to give me time to make that decision. I'll announce it to God at our meeting tonight."

"I hope and pray you become a believer in our God," Archangel Judy Lynn said. "If you do, and if God accepts you into paradise, we'll have peace and happiness in the universe. May God steer you toward the right decision."

"Thank you. I want to skip lunch and dinner so I can concentrate on my final decision. There's a lot riding on it."

"We'll leave you, then," Archangel Stan said. "Personally, it would be a pleasure to send you back to hell, where I believe you belong. If you need anything, call, and we'll assist you. Good-bye."

The two archangels left.

When they were back in their guard room, Archangel Stan called Jesus to inform him of Satan's conflict in making his final decision.

At nine o'clock that evening, Archangels Stan and Judy Lynn went to get Satan for his meeting with God and the religious leaders.

He looked like a movie star in his custom three-piece suit with black alligator belt and shiny black shoes. His face and hair were perfectly groomed, and his teeth were pearly white.

He smiled at Archangel Judy Lynn when they arrived. "How do I look?" he asked. "Will I win the hearts and minds of the ladies of the universe?"

She laughed. "You know you look good, and you're right. Some weak women will fall in love with you, but that won't be enough votes for you to win and let you stay in New Jerusalem."

"Is it all right if I speak with you alone for a moment?" Satan looked at Archangel Stan. "There's something I'd like to ask her."

"I have total confidence in her," Archangel Stan replied. "Does it have to do with your future here in paradise?"

"Absolutely. It's about our future here in paradise."

The archangel walked to the back of the cage and kept his eyes on the two of them, but he couldn't overhear what they said.

Satan looked into Archangel Judy Lynn's eyes. "We don't have much time to talk, so I'll get right to the point. I've been thinking about you, and I think I'm in love with you. I hope you have the same feelings for me."

She stepped back and hesitated before speaking. "I'm very attracted to you, and I like you a lot, but I don't think I'm in love with you. How do you know you won't be sent back to hell today?"

Archangel Stan returned and suddenly butted in. "I have a question for you, Satan. Have you decided if you're a good believer in God? Will you please give us an answer?" He looked at Archangel Judy Lynn. "Has he discussed any plans regarding paradise?"

She looked embarrassed. "We discussed personal business. It had nothing to do with paradise."

Satan's mood became serious. "I've made my decision about becoming a believer, but you'll have to wait for me to tell God. The whole universe will soon know what I decided."

They gathered all Satan's papers and items he needed for presenting his case before God.

"Turn around," Archangel Stan told him. "Put your hands behind your back."

Archangel Judy Lynn handcuffed Satan, and they escorted him to the portal that would transport them to God's headquarters in the church in St. Petersburg, Florida, at the corner of 71st Street and 38th Avenue.

Within minutes, Satan stood before the altar looking at God and all the religious leaders of the universe.

Archangels Stan and Judy Lynn stood on either side of Satan, holding his arms. They looked around the crowded church and recognized most of the renowned reporters from around the world who were assigned to cover the meeting between God and Satan. A TV camera at the back of the church televised the event for everyone in the universe.

God, banging his gavel, called the meeting to order. "Archangels, please uncuff Satan."

Archangel Judy Lynn released the handcuffs, then the two guard archangels stepped back and sat behind Satan, leaving him standing alone before God.

"Satan," God began, "we're glad to have you appear in person before the universe and our committee of religious leaders. Hopefully, we can come to an agreement to solve the universe's problems today. Do you have an opening statement?"

Satan looked around at the overcrowded church, then back at God. "God, I have an opening statement. If I may, I'll read it to you and the entire world."

He took out a document and tore it in half. "I don't need a prepared statement. I know exactly what I want to say."

God nodded. "Please proceed with your statement."

Satan approached the podium. "May it please God and the universe, what you hope to achieve is admirable—peace and happiness in the universe. All believers must know, though, that this is almost impossible unless you're living in a dream world. There will always be evildoers in the universe no matter what we agree to today. With my knowledge and expertise in evil, I can state that there is no way to stop it. You can slow evil down, but you'll never eliminate it. Evil will always be with us no matter what we do.

"God and all believers must realize that evil will always be with us. If I decide to join your God, we can control it to a level that we can all live with in the New Jerusalem."

"What do you mean, if you decide to join us?" God asked. "We decide if you're welcome to join us and live in New Jerusalem or if you'll be sent back to hell."

"It's still my choice to join you," Stan replied. "I can help you fulfill your dreams and the dreams of all believers to have peace and happiness in the universe, or I can go back to hell and start the demon movement all over again. I can create misery and chaos in the universe. All I have to do is give those demons the order, and it then becomes just a matter of time before you'll have the same problems you've always had. If we come to an agreement, we could work together and achieve peace and happiness in the world. It's Your call, God."

"How do I know I can trust you?" God asked angrily. "After dealing with you for millions of years, we've concluded your word isn't worth anything. Let me get this straight. Are you saying that you're the only one who can order the demons in hell to recreate evil in the universe?"

"God," Satan said proudly, "I have the power. No one else can give the order to create evil or have peace and happiness reign in the universe. You must take my word that I'll work with you to have paradise in the New Jerusalem. I can prove through my deeds and actions that I will keep my word."

Buddha stood to ask Satan, "You want us to take your word that you'll work for peace and happiness? Are you kidding me? I wouldn't trust you as far as I could throw you."

"Do you want to hear my plan for paradise or not?"

"Go ahead," God said. "Tell us your plan."

"I want to be restored to my former title of archangel. I can become a religious leader among the former demons and anyone else suspected of becoming a demon. I could help tutor them to believe in God and become good citizens. What do you think of that?"

"Let me play devil's advocate," God said. "What's to stop you from using the former demons and anyone we suspect of becoming a demon to start another army of demons to wage war against us?"

Satan smiled, knowing God caught him in the plan to use former demons to regain power and rule the new universe. He started with his first explanation of how God was wrong.

"I never thought about using my former demons to start an army against you. You'll have to take my word on that."

Moses stood. "Why should we pardon you for all the atrocities you committed over millions of years? You tortured and killed millions of believers and demons. Do you think we should forgive you for the crimes you committed and let you go without punishment?"

Satan was glad they stopped asking about the demon army. "Look, Moses, I know you're prejudiced against me for the crimes I did in World War Two, but you have to get over that. What do you want me to say? I'm sorry? OK. I'm sorry for the atrocities I committed. I hope all religious leaders who believe in forgiveness will forgive me."

Satan realized he didn't have any hope of winning an argument with the male religious leaders, so his attitude changed. He became more vocal in his argument with them.

"Tell the universe which of your accomplishment you're proud of," Jesus said.

Satan laughed. "I have a long list of the things I feel are noteworthy. Those who are watching this trial better sit down. This will take <u>a while.</u> Remember I have a different standard than you do.

"I invented and used the demon powers of greed, poverty, prejudice, and the total abuse of power. One of the things that I am very proud of recently is that I created one of the most deadly viruses in the history of the world. The corona virus! It has killed millions and millions of good believers and ruined the world economy. I created cancer, diabetes, and other diseases that kill and make believers suffer until they reach a painful death. I made my demon drug companies raise the prices on drugs they made, so they could profit from the suffering of good believers.

"Abortions were another doozy of mine. When I created that one, I realized I could pit all religions against each other and create chaos among believers. I was proud of that one.

"At the top of the list are wars, crimes, murders, mass shootings, and mass murders that destroyed thousands of good believers."

When he mentioned the sex slave business, he laughed, because he was glad, he made females into second-class citizens without any rights. He looked at the audience. "Women, you still don't have all your rights. I'm no longer in charge on Earth, either.

"I treated women badly, but what's the excuse for the religious leaders who still haven't given women their rights? Think about it. Women can't become priests or leaders of most churches. They're still treated as property in some religions. They need permission to get a divorce. They're told what to wear when they go outside the home. In some countries, they can't even drive cars."

<u>God</u> stood. "The law in the New Jerusalem is that women are equal in the eye of their God."

The women stood and gave God a loud cheer and applause.

Satan looked at God. "See? I'm not so bad. I just put pressure on you to change the law to give all women in the universe their equal rights."

"If you look at what I said two days ago, I already passed a law giving women equal rights."

"May I continue with my accomplishments?"

"We've heard enough. Let's have the next questioner."

"I want to make one other point about my accomplishments that will help the believers in the universe."

"All right. Finish your point, Satan."

"Thank You. My point is that I bring a lot to the table. When we demons put our minds to any plan, we finish it no matter how long it might take. I have had great success and experience in motivating demons to do the impossible in planning and succeeding in their evil ways.

"If I choose to join You and Your believers, I can give my demons the order to work with Your believers. I'm the only one in the universe with that power. I can guarantee that the demons will work with Your believers to achieve the plan for peace and happiness in the universe.

"The only thing I ask in return is for us to be set free from hell. Then all will live in harmony in the universe. Otherwise, if and when I return to hell, I'll give the order to my demons to wage endless war on You and Your believers again. What do You say to that?"

"We'll discuss your proposal in the jury room," God replied. "Let's proceed with the questioning. Next, I wish to call upon our distinguished women religious leaders."

All three of them asked variations of the same question. "When you were taken into custody, you looked frail and decrepit. How'd you get so healthy and good-looking?"

Joyce Meyer asked questions that tried to determine if Satan was lying or telling the truth.

Satan looked her in the eye and replied, "I'm a victim. If you can see it in your heart to grant me mercy and forgiveness, I would always support you."

The more pointed the questions Joyce had, the more Satan answered, and the more it became obvious that Satan was lying about working with God and His believers to achieve peace and happiness in the universe.

It was clear that Satan never said he would stop his demons from causing more misery in the world. It slowly became clear that he hadn't changed. He was trying to fool God and the good believers into thinking he no longer had a plan to rule the world, but he was clearly lying.

The questions and answers lasted another two hours. It was obvious by the end that Satan hadn't changed.

God struck His gavel. "We have enough information to make a sound decision about Satan's faith. All religious leaders will meet me in the rectory to render our verdict within one hour. We must have a unanimous vote."

Chapter
FOURTEEN

Satan Returns to His Cage

Satan was handcuffed and brought back to his cage, guarded by Archangels Stan and Judy Lynn. Satan, in a jovial mood, made small talk with Judy.

"How do you think I did answering all those questions?" Satan asked.

"I have some bad news for you," she replied. "You did terrible. You didn't convince anyone that you're a true believer. We should organize a going-away party for when you're sent to hell."

Archangel Stan laughed. "To tell you the truth, I, for one, won't miss you. Please give my regards to the demons in hell when you get there."

Satan looked at them. "We'll see about that," he said sternly. "I'll bet you that the religious leaders let me stay here.

"Remember, it must be a unanimous decision, just like in criminal trials in the United States. There are three women on that committee, and I need to get only one of them to change her vote. That's why I wanted to be as handsome as possible, so women couldn't resist me. I doubt anyone at that meeting realized I was playing up to the women religious leaders. At least one of them is attracted to me."

Archangel Stan gave him a glare. "You've got a bet. You don't have any appeal to me. You're as guilty as sin."

Archangel Judy Lynn became serious. "The more I think about how the meeting went, the more I think there are at least two women religious leaders who were attracted to you. I could tell by the way they looked at you and asked their questions. When you answered the last question from a male religious leader, you acted differently than when you spoke to the women."

Archangel Judy Lynn remembered that one of the women, right before beginning her questions, checked her mirror to fix her makeup and add some dark-red lipstick. She pulled her blouse tighter and released the top two buttons to show more of her cleavage.

"I think one of them is attracted to you," Archangel Judy Lynn said.

He turned to Archangel Stan. "Still want to make that bet?"

They left Satan making final arrangements for a hung jury and to tell Jesus what they learned about Satan's plans. Archangel called Jesus and gave him the details of Satan's strategy to create a hung jury.

Jesus thanked them for the information. "I'll relay it to God and the religious leaders."

Jesus quickly called God to explain what he found out.

"My Son," God said, "I know who that woman is. I won't disclose her name, but I'll ask if she has a crush on Satan. If she admits it, I'll excuse her from jury duty for bias."

"What about the other jurists? Will you ask them the same thing about being biased toward Satan?"

"Yes. I'll ask all of them the same question before I swear them in as a jury."

Jesus hung up knowing that God would handle the situation.

God walked into the jury room to meet them and give instructions about reaching a fair verdict on *Satan v. the Universe*.

"Before I swear you in as jurors, I have a question," God said. "Is there anyone here who feels prejudiced or biased for or against Satan? If you are, please excuse yourselves."

All three women religious leaders raised their hands and stood.

"Thank you," God said. "You're excused from jury duty."

They left the room.

God looked around and saw more hands raised by those who wished to be excused from jury duty. "Anyone else who feels prejudiced in this case is excused from jury duty. You may leave the room."

God was left with twenty-four jurors, which was more than enough to decide Satan's fate. "Raise your right hands." God administered the oath to them.

"Archangel Dave, Jr., will be in charge of any needs you might have," God said. "If you wish to examine any evidence, put the request in writing, and give it to him. He'll be stationed just outside the door. I will now leave you to deliberate on your verdict."

God left the room.

During an hour of deliberations, Archangel Dave, Jr. sat in front of the door and heard the soft muttering of voices behind it. The more time the jury talked, the louder the voices became, until some were shouting. It was clear that at least a handful of the religious leaders wanted to give Satan a chance to become a good believer and work with God to achieve peace and happiness in the universe.

Those who held out to find Satan guilty argued that it was their golden opportunity finally to rid the universe of evil.

Most of the religious leaders were able to show that Satan was lying. No one with a sound mind would believe anything he said. Even more importantly, they said that if Satan was allowed to remain in the New Jerusalem and turned out to be lying, the entire universe would return to having wars and misery. They didn't want to risk it.

The arguments behind the closed door became heated. Archangel Dave, Jr. finally knocked and stepped inside. "May I suggest that the jury take a lunch break and relax? I'll bring in your meal, if that's OK."

"You must have read our minds," one leader said. "A lunch break is a good idea. Please bring it in."

After he brought in the lunch, he sat outside the closed door again and heard the members talking and laughing. It seemed they were calming down and were able to get along again.

An hour later, they called him in to retrieve the remains of their lunch. He entered a room that had the atmosphere of a college fraternity room, with people getting along fabulously.

One hour later, Archangel Dave, Jr. heard a knock on the door and opened it. Mohammed handed him a written note signed by all jurors.

"We have reached a verdict," he told Archangel Dave, Jr. "Please give our note to God."

Archangel Dave, Jr. accepted the note. "Thank you." He bowed his head in respect and closed the door. He waited a moment to make sure no one could surprise him, then he opened the note and read it, feeling suddenly confused. He realized he was the only one in the universe who knew the verdict until he gave the note to God.

He called Jesus to tell Him to bring more archangels to guard the church for security once God called the meeting back into session.

"I'll notify the news reporters, too," Jesus said.

God made all the arrangements to have the reading of the verdict run as smoothly as possible. Such a procedure took at least three hours.

The church was again packed to capacity, with standing room only. Reporters from around the universe and the lucky good believers who were inside prepared themselves to witness history being made.

God entered the church and walked down the aisle with His entourage and aides. At the altar, he turned to walk to the podium.

"Let us pray," God said, "and recite the Lord's Prayer."

All good believers in the universe were silent as they prayed. Afterward, God asked the audience to be seated while the verdict was read aloud.

"The religious leaders who compose the jury have reached a verdict," God said. "I want to ask all who are in attendance to be quiet before and after the verdict is announced." He looked at one of his aides. "Have the archangels bring Satan in."

A few minutes later, Satan was brought before the altar to face God and the good believers. The jury slowly filed in, as the church stood and waited respectfully. Once they sat down, God told the attendees to sit.

Archangel Stan left Satan and walked to the altar with his head bowed before handing the verdict sheet to God.

God read the verdict, and His expression changed. He looked at it again, then he looked at the jury, handing the sheet to his aide. "Make sure this is authentic," he whispered.

Each juror quickly read the page and nodded that it was accurate. Finally, they handed it back to the aide, who brought it to God.

God read it one more time, then said, "Before I announce the verdict, I have some questions for Satan.

"You said you were the only one who could control the evil demons, and that they took orders only from you, correct?"

Satan was stunned by the question. Was God trying to ensure himself that Satan was the only one who could stop the evil by giving orders to the demons?

"Yes," Satan said. "They can take orders only from me."

"How do you communicate your orders to them?"

"I can only give orders directly, face-to-face. All my orders are given at meeting with my generals, always face-to-face."

"I want to be crystal clear about how you give your evil plans. You and you alone must speak to your generals to have them fulfill your orders? Is that correct?"

"With all due respect, God, what are you getting at? If you want me to promise I'll give the order at our next meeting, telling my demons to work with all believers for peace and happiness, I will. I give you my word on that. I'd do it right now, but I can't. The believers have to hear my voice and see me in person to fulfill my orders. I know that makes it hard to get anything done. It would be much easier to text, email, or call them, but they must see me and hear my words directly to fulfill my orders. I hope that answers your questions."

"You did. Do you have anything to say before I announce your verdict?"

Satan smiled and confidently faced the jury. "I know all members of the jury believe in forgiveness and redemption. I'm counting on your true beliefs that you will forgive me for all the evil I have done.

"I look forward to working with all good believers to achieve peace and happiness in the universe. Could you imagine what will happen when they hear my voice, and I order them to work with God and the good believers to work for peace and happiness? We'll achieve paradise!

"I want to conclude that I promise to go to confession and ask God for His forgiveness, too. I want to thank the jury for letting me stay in New Jerusalem where we can all work together."

"Are you finished with your statement?" God asked.

"Yes."

"Archangels Stan and Judy Lynn, release the handcuffs."

Satan smiled, thinking that was a good thing. The two archangels began to relax, thinking Satan was found guilty after all, and he would not be allowed to stay in New Jerusalem.

"Thank you," God told the archangels. "Please be seated and leave Satan standing alone while I read the verdict."

The archangels sat in the front row, as a hush fell over the church.

Satan smiled, knowing his lies worked. The minute he was set free, he would begin his plan to become the evil master of the universe and rule it with an iron fist. His first act of freedom would be to give orders to the former demons who lived in New Jerusalem. That would allow him to take over and control the world.

Once that was accomplished, he would find a way to reverse the black hole and bring back all the demons to wage war on the good believers. The religious leaders were incredibly naïve to think they could change demons. That never worked. Demons always remained demons. That was the way of the universe.

Satan laughed softly.

"What are you laughing at?" God asked.

"I heard a joke one of your archangels told me. It just came back to me."

God looked at the expectant audience. "Please take your seats and be quiet while I read the verdict."

He waited a moment, then read, "We, they jury of good believers, find Satan *nolo contendere.*"

People immediately began whispering, asking each other what that meant. Only lawyers and those with legal minds understood. The Internet immediately crashed, as millions of people tried to ask Google what the term was.

Satan rocked back on his heels. "What does that mean?"

God knew what it meant. It meant Satan wasn't found guilty or not guilty, but he was still subject to punishment as if he were guilty. God understood that the religious leaders couldn't find Satan guilty, because they all taught that sinners could be redeemed. Some of them would never find Satan guilty.

The verdict must have been a compromise.

"Quiet, please," God said, waiting until the hubbub died down. He turned to Satan. "Is there anything you want to say before I pronounce sentence on you?"

Satan, feeling shocked and confused, asked, "What does *nolo contendere* mean? Am I guilty or not? Does that mean you're sending me back to hell, or can I stay in New Jerusalem?"

God looked at him for a moment. "For all intents and purposes, Satan, it means you're guilty of all the crimes and atrocities you committed against mankind. That means you can be punished."

Archangels Stan and Judy Lynn immediately stood and walked behind Satan to prevent any attempt at flight.

Satan slowly regained his composure, then he became angry and cursed God. "Since you can't kill me, because I'm still an archangel, then the only thing you can do is send me to where I came from. That's no problem. I never stopped planning to become the evil leader of the universe. In fact, the war against all good believers never stopped.

"I'll tell you exactly how I feel now. Once You send me back to hell, you and all the good believers in the universe will face total war. I'll mobilize my demons to wage war against You and anyone who stands with you. I promise I won't stop the war until I rule the universe."

God stopped his tirade. "We've heard enough about your plans against us. First, I want the archangel guards to walk the prisoner to the window and let him see all that the good believers have accomplished in the last five days to create paradise in New Jerusalem."

Archangels Stan and Judy Lynn placed the handcuffs on Satan's wrists and walked him to the large window before pulling aside the curtains. Bright light spilled, illuminating the church.

Everyone in the church and viewing on the Internet saw the progress that had been made. They stared at a beautiful blue sky, and scenery that matched what the archangels had in heaven, with tall, crystal-clear waterfalls. It reminded all the archangels, including Satan, of the Garden of Eden that existed in heaven.

He saw the good believers outside, reading books, and children playing in the grass, laughing and enjoying themselves. Couples held hands and kissed. Families had picnics in the beautiful parks. Satan felt the total peace, love, and happiness those people enjoyed and recalled when he was an archangel and grew up in heaven with the same feeling.

He recalled the good days in heaven, and he remembered how he loved living there. Suddenly, he felt guilty for all the evil he did and the suffering he caused.

Satan stared out the window for over five minutes, dreaming of the past, and how he let greed drive to control the universe lead him to do evil.

God signaled the guards to bring Satan back to be sentenced and punished. The archangels pulled him back before the altar.

Satan looked up at God. "You're right, and I'm wrong. I want You to punish me, because I deserve it for doing all that evil to the good believers for so many years. I now have a plan that will allow peace and happiness for the entire universe for eternity."

"What's your plan?" God asked.

"Since you can't kill me, because I'm an archangel, and no one can replace me as the head of my evil empire, if You can prevent me from communicating with my demons, they will eventually disappear from the universe. There will be no other leader of evil. You will win and will gain paradise throughout the universe.

"I don't know how you can stop me from communicating to my demons. I haven't figured that out yet."

God thought for a moment. "Are you sure that's what you want to be your punishment, to be silent for the rest of eternity? I can have that done."

"God, I made my decision to help you achieve peace and happiness for all good believers. I just asked if you could see it in your heart to forgive me for my sins."

"I will forgive you, Satan. Is there anything else I can do for you before I silence you for eternity?"

"No, my God."

God ordered the two guard archangels to release Satan's handcuffs. They left him standing alone before God.

"Are you ready to be silenced?" God asked.

"Yes, my God." He raised his hands over his head and bowed, then began saying the Lord's Prayer.

Total silence filled the church and the universe. Everyone wondered what would happen.

A small bolt of lightning struck Satan's right temple, knocking him unconscious to the floor, where he lay without moving. The archangel guards ran up to assist him, but Satan was in a deep coma. There was nothing they could do to help him. He had entered a vegetative state where he would remain for eternity.

God stood at the podium. "He will be in a coma for the rest of eternity, unable to communicate with his demons. I never thought I would say this, but I want to thank Satan for his help in achieving paradise in New Jerusalem and the universe. All the demons are now neutralized. We don't need to fear them anymore.

"To all My good believers, please enjoy your lives in paradise. Your God will always be there for you and your families. God will always protect you and your family from evil. Always trust in your God and follow your religion.

"God bless all My followers!"

www.ingramcontent.com/pod-product-compliance
Lightning Source LLC
Chambersburg PA
CBHW071858070526
44583CB00016B/1747